AF575384

THE FOUNDATIONS OF WISDOM

VOLUME 2

PHILOSOPHY OF NATURE

THE FOUNDATIONS OF WISDOM

VOLUME 2

PHILOSOPHY OF NATURE

FR. SEBASTIAN WALSHE, O. PRAEM.

TAN Books
Gastonia, North Carolina

Cover design by Andrew Schmalen

Library of Congress Control Number: 2022948331

ISBN: 978-1-5051-2639-6
Kindle ISBN: 978-1-5051-3065-2
ePUB ISBN: 978-1-5051-3066-9

Published in the United States by
TAN Books
PO Box 269
Gastonia, NC 28053
www.TANBooks.com

Printed in the United States of America

CONTENTS

Preface: Hunting for Happiness . . . . *vii*

Introduction 1

1 The Place of Natural Philosophy among the Arts and Sciences 2

2 What We Are Looking for in Natural Philosophy. . . .10

3 The Method to Follow in Natural Philosophy 15

4 Is Motion Even Possible? 21

5 The Principles of Change in All Natural Things 27

6 Substantial Change, Substantial Form, and Prime Matter .31

7 The Definition of Nature 44

8 The Four Causes Used for Demonstration in Natural Philosophy 49

9 The Argument for Materialist Evolution 55

10 Critiquing the Argument for Materialist Evolution . . 60

11 The Definition of Motion 74

12 The Measures of Motion 82

13 The Divisibility of Motion and Mobile 92

14 Where Does Natural Philosophy Lead Us? 95

15 Demonstrations for the Existence of God 110

Appendix: Are Living Organisms Just Machines? *120*

PREFACE

Hunting for Happiness

The discovery and development of philosophy is part of man's larger search for happiness. As man was hunting for happiness, he found philosophy. Much of human ingenuity and energy was originally directed towards removing the obstacles to happiness: for example, the arts of hunting and agriculture were developed to alleviate hunger; the art of housebuilding was developed to alleviate the suffering associated with excessive heat and cold; various martial arts and weapons were developed to protect against violence from animals and other men; medicine was developed to cure illness. But once these arts had been developed, and man had time for leisure, it became apparent that there exists in man a more fundamental desire than food, clothing, and bodily health. It is a desire not merely to avoid evils, but a desire for some positive good, and it is a desire for a positive good which is not merely instrumental to something else (such as practical knowledge), but a good desired for its own sake. Aristotle expressed this desire simply in the statement: "All men by nature desire to know."

It may seem strange that happiness should have much to do with knowledge. After all, very few men dedicate real effort and time to searching for knowledge. What knowledge they do search for tends to be practical in nature: that is, it is for the sake of making or doing things. And yet, it is an indisputable fact of history that once the chief practical arts had been established, and the needs of the body provided for, men naturally turned to philosophy in their leisure time. Aristotle recounts that "after all such arts had been developed, those sciences were pursued which are sought neither for the sake of pleasure nor necessity. This happened in places where men had leisure. Hence the mathematical arts originated in Egypt where the priestly class was permitted leisure."[1] And again: "When nearly all the things necessary for life, leisure and learning were acquired, this kind of prudence began to be sought."[2] But if this is so, how do we account for the fact that so few people consider knowledge to be essential for happiness?

This question is like the question of why so few children prefer a high paying job or an excellent education to ice cream. First of all, since the goods of the body are better known than the goods of the soul, it is natural that men should seek to provide for the goods of the body first. Secondly, happiness is not found in the possession and exercise of just any knowledge, but only in the best knowledge, and this is very difficult to achieve. Just as it would be impossible for a child to perform well at a high paying job or to receive an excellent education all at once, so it would be impossible for someone to acquire and use the knowledge needed for happiness without first passing through years of experience and study. Finally, notice that Aristotle did not say all men by nature desire to *come to* know, but rather that all men by nature desire to know. Samuel Johnson once famously quipped about seeing a famous landmark in Ireland that it was "worth seeing . . . but not worth going to see." There is a similar relationship

---

1 *Metaphysics* 981b22-24 (independent confirmation of the leisure afforded the priestly class in Egypt is found in Gn 47:22).

2 *Metaphysics* 982b22-23.

between knowing and coming to know. Coming to know can be arduous and even painful. But if you asked the man on the street whether he would like to know some important truth if it took no effort, I suppose nearly everyone would say yes. As it is, because many obstacles stand in the way of possessing knowledge, there are few who seek it.

So philosophy is near the end of man's search for happiness. But even within philosophy itself there is an order of discovery which naturally arises from the search for happiness. For we want to know the supreme good of man, but to know that we need to know what man is, and since man is a natural being, we need to know what nature is. So philosophers began to examine nature. But once these things had been worked out in outline, it became clear that the nature of man is difficult to know, that it is even difficult to know about the existence and nature of the soul, and that the highest perfection of the human soul, wisdom, is even more difficult to know. Therefore, it was necessary to develop one final art: logic, which assists us in coming to know difficult truths well. Plato's Socrates seems to have been the first to acknowledge a need for an "art about arguments" in the *Phaedo*, precisely as he is searching to discover the existence and nature of the human soul.

The order of discovery in philosophy is almost inverse to the order in which philosophy should be learned. First, students should study logic, which is the art that treats of acquiring the good of speculative reason: truth. Since every science searches for truth, logic teaches how to proceed correctly in every science. Second, they should study mathematics, which among the sciences is the easiest in which to find certitude (hence there is much agreement in this part of philosophy). Third, they should study natural things (natural philosophy). Fourth, among natural things, they should focus their study upon living things, especially man (the study of the soul). Fifth, once they know accurately the nature of man, and the various powers and perfections of the soul, they should study the good for man (ethics). And since man's supreme good consists in knowing things better than himself, the philosopher should study the first cause of all being (wisdom or metaphysics) last.[3] For the very exercise of knowing these things higher than man is the happiness which man desires. That is, natural happiness consists in contemplating the truths which are the conclusions of metaphysics.

Because this is only an introduction to philosophy, this text will not consider the last part of philosophy (metaphysics). Such a consideration belongs not to the beginning student, but to an advanced student. Moreover, because the science of mathematics is widely taught, and much easier than the other parts of philosophy, this text will not consider that part of philosophy either. Perhaps the best elementary treatment of mathematics according to its proper method can be found in Euclid's *Elements*.

Finally, this text will not proceed by a primarily historical method, as is typical in most introductions to philosophy. The order of history in philosophy is not necessarily a progression from ignorance to knowledge or error to truth. It is quite possible for an earlier philosopher to know more than a later one. Nor is the order of history necessarily the best order for the beginning student to follow if he is in search of truth. This text does not seek to inform the student about the positions taken by various philosophers, but rather to lay out the method best suited to human nature of coming to understand the order among the ultimate causes of reality. We study the Pythagorean theorem not to know what

---

[3] This order of study is laid out by St. Thomas Aquinas at the beginning of his *Commentary on Aristotle's Nicomachean Ethics* and at the beginning of his *Commentary on the Book of Causes*.

Pythagoras thought, but because it is true and worth knowing. It would be worthwhile to study the same theorem even if it was discovered by Frankie Watkins. In philosophy, we are not so much concerned with who discovered some truth as with the truth itself, and how it can be known. While much of what is found in this text will be truths discovered by Aristotle and Saint Thomas Aquinas, they stand on their own and do not rely upon the authority of those who first discovered and presented them.

Introduction

In the first quarter of this introduction to philosophy, we studied logic, the art of reasoning well, in order to acquire the basic tools necessary for demonstration. Logic, like any tool, is therefore meant to be used for the sake of something else, something better than itself. In this quarter we will begin to make use of the tools we acquired in logic in order to come to know truths about the natural world in a rigorous and scientific way.

CHAPTER 1

The Place of Natural Philosophy among the Arts and Sciences

Practical and Speculative Truth

Not all truths are equal. Some true things are good to know because of something we can make or do with those truths. For example, it is good to know a recipe or a phone number in order to make a cake or to call a friend. In themselves, the recipe or the phone number do not perfect you as a human being. In fact, we would think it strange or even disordered if someone were to read a phone book just for the sake of memorizing the numbers, without any intention to call them. Their goodness is completely relative to the thing you can make or do with them. We call such truths *practical truths*: that which is known for the sake of making or doing something.

Now since everything useful is useful for something better than itself, it must follow that the best things of all are useless. That is, they must be good for their own sake, and not for the sake of anything better than themselves: they are the best things. To be useless is not the same as being worthless. In the order of knowledge, we call these best truths *speculative truths*: those which are known for their own sake, not for any other reason. Speculative truths in themselves perfect you as a human being—to know them makes you a better man, a more perfect man.

One of the customs of modern men is to value knowledge to the extent that it is practical: "Knowledge is power," one famous adage states. But this custom does not stand up to close scrutiny. Practical knowledge is a knowledge to produce order in something. But any order produced by human reason is less perfect than human reason, since the cause of a thing is more perfect than the effect (for nothing gives what it does not have). Hence, it follows that practical knowledge cannot perfect human reason. On the other hand, speculative knowledge is derived from an order already found in things. And since this order proceeds from the divine mind (as we shall show at the end of this quarter), it follows that the order discovered by human reason in things can perfect the human mind by uniting the human mind with a mind greater than itself.

From this we can see that speculative truths are better and more conducive to perfecting a man than practical truths. Hence, it is the speculative truths (truths good to know for their own sake) that are to be valued as having the highest worth and dignity.

The Place of Natural Philosophy in the Whole Body of Knowledge

In the first quarter, we drew up a roadmap of all things that can be known. It is time to return to that roadmap to identify where natural philosophy fits among the things that we can know.

Recall: Everything that can be known has an order. But order is related to reason in three ways. There is:

1. the order produced by reason (the arts or practical sciences);
2. the order discovered by reason (the speculative sciences); and
3. the order revealed to reason (sacred theology).

Since natural philosophy regards the order found in the natural world, natural philosophy obviously concerns the order discovered by reason in things. Hence, natural philosophy is one of the speculative sciences. For example, we find in the natural world that the immature always comes before the mature, as a boy before a man, or a puppy before a dog. That's an order already found in things, not something we put there. But there are also other sciences concerned with the order found in things, such as mathematics. How is natural philosophy separated from these other sciences?

One way to determine the different kinds of reasoned-out knowledge (science) is to see what kinds of definitions are used in arguing to the conclusions of that reasoned-out knowledge. Remember that we discovered in the first volume that science is the conclusion to a demonstration, and every demonstration has a definition as its middle term. Hence, if I have a different kind of definition, I will have a different kind of conclusion or science. Let's take an example: If I were to define a triangle or a circle, would I be right to include some kind of material, such as metal or wood, in the definition? No. Mathematical triangles and circles are not made of wood or metal or any particular kind of matter. I might find a wooden or metal triangle somewhere, but the particular material would not be part of what it means to be a triangle. On the other hand, when I define natural things, like horses, trees, or gold, I see that the material out of which they are made is essential to what they are. Flesh and bones are essential to horses: without them a horse would not truly be a horse. Wood is essential to trees. Metal is essential to gold. So I can say that the science of mathematics is different from natural philosophy in this way: the subjects studied in mathematics are not defined with any matter, but the subjects of natural philosophy are defined with some kind of definite matter.

There is also another speculative science called metaphysics (which means after or beyond the physical). This science is about immaterial substances like angels and God. We will prove the existence of immaterial substances later on, but for now let's take it for granted that such immaterial beings can exist. How then would we distinguish mathematics from metaphysics? Both are about things which are defined without matter. A mathematical triangle is defined without matter, and so is an angel, so what's the difference? One important difference between the subjects studied in mathematics and metaphysics is that the subjects of mathematics are quantities, and those quantities cannot exist on their own. They have to exist in something else, namely a substance. And the substance in which these mathematical subjects exist are material. So the subjects studied in mathematics exist in matter, even though they are defined without matter. On the other hand, angels and God are substances. They exist on their own. So they are defined without matter *and* they exist without matter.

In summary, we can say that the three speculative sciences are distinguished in this way: natural philosophy is about things which exist in matter and are defined with matter; mathematics is about things which exist in matter, but are defined without matter; and metaphysics is about things which exist without matter and are defined without matter. This is represented in the figure on the next page.

	Exists in Matter	Exists without Matter
Defined with Matter	Natural philosophy: Things which exist in matter and are defined with matter (men, horses, trees, minerals, etc.)	
Defined without Matter	Mathematics: Things which exist in matter but are defined without matter (triangles, circles, cubes, etc.)	Metaphysics: Things which exist without matter and are defined without matter (angels and God)

Figure 1

By the way, notice that there is a fourth logical possibility: a science about that which exists without matter, but is defined with matter. Why don't we have four speculative sciences? Because while something which exists without matter and is defined with matter is a logical possibility, it is not a *real* possibility.[4] The reason that it is not a real possibility is because the human mind is immaterial, so it is able to consider material things without matter, but it cannot consider immaterial things as if they had matter. Being immaterial itself, the human mind can consider things in an immaterial way. The fact that the human mind is immaterial is something we shall prove at the end of third quarter.

[4] A helpful example to illustrate the difference between a logical and real possibility can be taken from mathematics. Let us divide up straight-sided geometrical figures into those which are closed and those which are open. Again, let us divide these into those with three or more sides and those with two or fewer sides. There are, therefore, four logical possibilities: (1) closed with three or more sides (for example, a triangle or a square); (2) open with three or more sides (for example, a figure in which one of the sides is missing, leaving it open); (3) open with two or fewer sides (for example, an angle); and (4) closed with two or fewer sides. This fourth logical possibility is not a *real* possibility, since two straight lines cannot enclose an area.

But when we say that the human mind considers material things without matter, doesn't this mean that these definitions are false? For example, isn't it false to define a triangle without matter? The answer is that it is one thing to consider A apart from B, and another thing to say that A exists apart from B. For example, I can consider my dad without considering his weight. When I think about whether I should love my dad, I would normally think about that without considering his weight. For that matter, I don't consider his height, the number of hairs on his head, or many other things that have nothing to do with whether or not I should love my father. By considering my dad without considering his weight, height, etc., I have not asserted that he does not have weight or height. This would be to say something false. I simply see that those other things are unimportant and do not need to be considered in determining whether I should love my dad. Similarly, it is possible to consider certain shapes like circles and triangles and squares without considering the matter of the things in which they are found. When I prove that a triangle has interior angles equal to two right angles (180 degrees), it is not important to determine what kind of matter this triangle is made of. So I consider that triangle without considering its matter. That is not to assert that there are triangles existing in the world that have no matter. This would be false.

In summary, we can say that natural philosophy is a speculative science (i.e., a reasoned-out knowledge about an order which reason discovers in things). In addition, natural philosophy is the speculative science about things which exist in matter and are defined with matter. The place of natural philosophy in the whole body of knowledge is schematically represented in the figure on the following page.

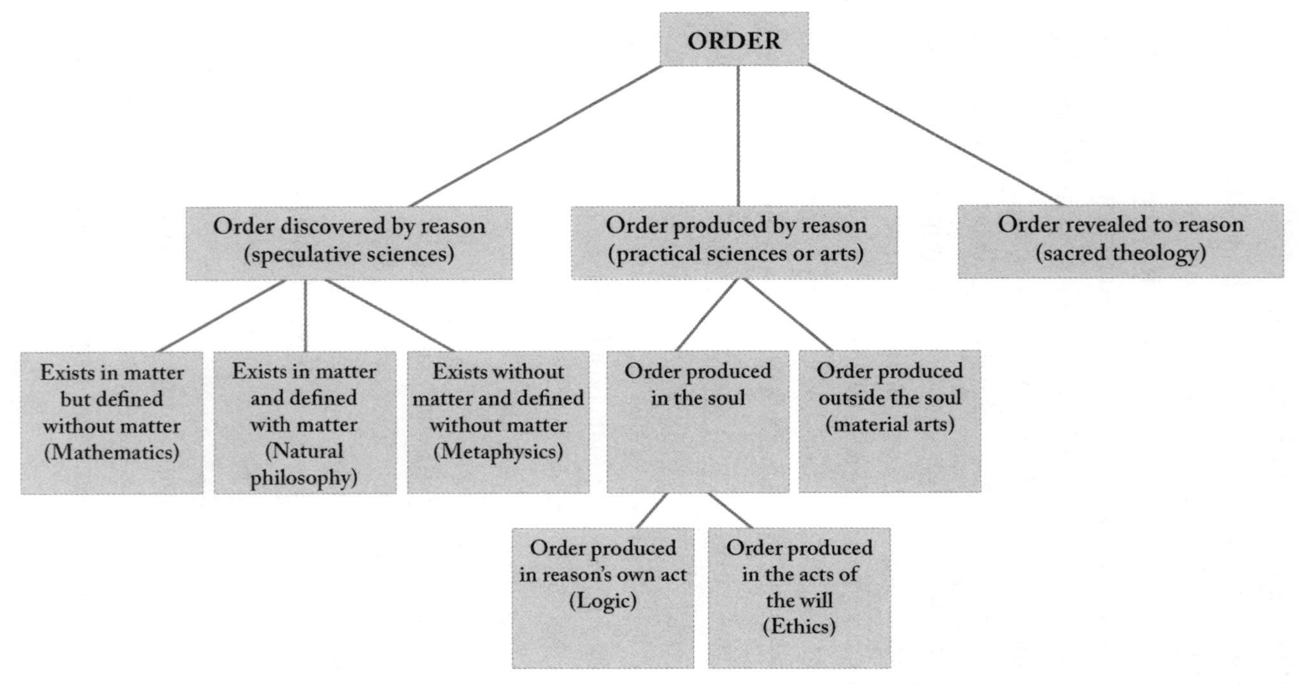

ORDER
Order discovered by reason (speculative sciences)
Order produced by reason (practical sciences or arts)
Order revealed to reason (sacred theology)
Exists in matter but defined without matter (Mathematics)
Exists in matter and defined with matter (Natural philosophy)
Exists without matter and defined without matter (Metaphysics)
Order produced in the soul
Order produced outside the soul (material arts)
Order produced in reason's own act (Logic)
Order produced in the acts of the will (Ethics)

Figure 2

Summary

- Natural philosophy is a speculative science, which means that it is knowledge worth knowing for its own sake, not merely as a means to some useful product.
- Speculative science is better than practical science since it perfects the human mind and is a kind of participation in the divine wisdom.
- This is because speculative science involves discovering an order which is in things, not an order put there by the human mind.
- Natural philosophy is about things which exist in matter and are defined with matter.

CHAPTER 2

What We Are Looking for in Natural Philosophy

The Subject of Natural Philosophy[5]

The subject of natural philosophy is what natural philosophy is about. More precisely, it is the subject about which we demonstrate some conclusion. Let's take an example that should be familiar from our logic course last quarter:

Man is a rational animal

Rational animals are capable of geometry

Therefore, man is capable of geometry

Here the conclusion is "man is capable of geometry." The grammatical subject of this statement in the conclusion is "man." So here we have reasoned to a conclusion about man, in which some property (e.g., "capable of geometry") is demonstrated to belong to the subject "man." Similarly, in natural philosophy, we will reason to a number of conclusions in which a property is demonstrated to belong to some subject.

But what is the subject in the science of natural philosophy? A simple and straightforward answer is: natural things, of course! But

[5] Supplementary text: St. Thomas, *Commentary on the Physics*, I.1, n.1-4.

what is a natural thing? Perhaps if we contrast a natural thing with its opposite, we can see better what a natural thing is. Natural things are opposed to artificial things. Artificial things are man-made. They do not grow or come into existence on their own, but only as a result of human thought and effort. In contrast, the natural thing comes to be all by itself, without needing any help from human thought or effort.[6] Both the artificial thing and the natural thing are made up of matter, but matter has within itself the inclination to become a natural thing, while matter does not have within itself the inclination to become an artificial thing: the artificial thing comes to be because of external forces, not internal inclinations. Take a bed, for example. There is no positive inclination within the wood to take the form of a bed. Rather, the natural thing that is wood has the positive inclination to take the form of a tree. Aristotle explains this by saying that motion which originates from an internal cause is "natural motion" while motion which originates from an external cause is "violent or unnatural motion."[7] To move wood to take the form of a bed requires some external force acting upon the wood in such a way that it artificially is turned into something it would never become by moving solely according to its source of internal motion, its nature. A bed has no internal principle of motion and so will not move on its own, but if pushed out a window or down a flight of stairs, it most certainly will. A baseball or a rock has no internal principle of motion to make it go up in the air, but if acted upon externally by someone throwing it, it certainly will.

We should observe, however, that artificial things are ultimately made up of natural things. If there were no trees, there could

[6] Supplementary text: C. S. Lewis, *Miracles*, ch. 2 (on the definition of nature).

[7] Supplementary text: Aristotle, *Physics*, Book VIII, ch. 4. NB: "Unnatural motion" is put in this way to indicate that the motion is not originating from the very nature of the thing being moved.

be no wooden beds. So art piggy-backs on nature. Therefore, when an artificial thing moves on its own (for example, when a knife falls), this is not insofar as it is artificial, but insofar as it is composed of something natural (the falling of the knife is due to the natural iron within it).

In conclusion we can say that the subject of natural philosophy is that which has within itself a source of motion and coming into existence.

Looking for the Principles, Causes, and Elements of Natural Things

In every science about something, one of the things we look for is whether or not this thing has principles, causes, or elements. If it does, then part of the job of a science is to come to know these principles, causes, and elements. So if natural things, things which have within themselves a source of motion and coming into existence, have principles, causes, or elements, natural philosophy will look for them. We have already seen how the first philosophers tried to do this when attempting to account for the natural world. Thales, for example, thought that the element that made up all natural things was water. Heraclitus thought that it was fire. Empedocles thought that there were multiple elements: earth, air, fire, and water. These thinkers also posited principles and causes besides the elements. For example, Empedocles thought that love and strife were principles and causes of the changes found in the natural world.

Let's begin our search by more precisely stating what we mean by principles, causes, and elements. A *principle* (we could also call it a "beginning") is *the first thing from which something is or comes to be*. For example, the starting point of a race is the principle of the race; the principle of a plant is the seed from which it grows. A *cause* is *that upon which something depends for its being or coming to be*. For example, the cause of a fight is anger, the cause of a statue is the marble out of which it is carved, the cause of the radii of a circle being equal is the shape of the circle, the cause of a business contract is the wealth both parties hope to acquire through it. We shall see later on that there are different kinds of causes for natural things. Finally, an *element* can be defined as *the first material cause of a thing which is indivisible as regards the kind of thing it is.*

That last definition is difficult, so let's take some time to understand it better. Take the example of concrete. Is concrete an element? It's a material cause of other things, but it is itself made up of sand, cement, and water. So concrete isn't an element, since it is not the *first* material cause out of which things are made. Not only that, but if you divide up concrete, you get three different kinds of things: sand, cement, and water. For something to be an element, it would have to be the first material cause of a thing and it would not be able to be divided into different kinds of other material. Today chemists have identified more than one hundred elements, which are usually represented on a chart called the "periodic table." Some elements found on that chart are hydrogen, oxygen, carbon, and gold. The first thing to see about these elements is that they are material causes of other things. Hydrogen and oxygen, for example, come together to make up water. Not only that, they are the *first* material causes of those other things. There are not some other kinds of substances that makes up hydrogen and oxygen. Thus, water cannot be an element since it is composed of prior substances (namely hydrogen and oxygen). In contrast, when you divide hydrogen and oxygen, you just get smaller and smaller packets of hydrogen and oxygen. Hydrogen and oxygen are divisible, but not *as regards the kinds of things they are.*

Someone might object: hydrogen and oxygen can be divided into protons, neutrons, and electrons. If protons, neutrons, and electrons were independent substances, able to exist on their own, then *they* would be the elements, rather than hydrogen, oxygen, carbon, etc. But it appears that protons, neutrons, and electrons are not able to exist in a stable way on their own: it seems that they exist only as parts of something else, not as independent substances, so for that reason chemists do not call them elements.

Looking at these three things again—principles, causes, and elements—we notice a relationship among them. All elements are causes (but not vice-versa). For example, oxygen is an element of water, and it is also a cause of water. But anger is a cause of a fight, yet it is not an element of the fight, since anger is not some kind of material. Again, all causes are principles (but not vice-versa). For example, anger is a principle of a fight since it is the first thing from which the fight comes to be, and it is also the cause of a fight, since the coming to be of the fight depended upon the anger of the one who started it. But the starting point of the race is a principle of the race, without being a cause of it, since the race does not depend upon the starting point (though in some way the racetrack does depend upon that starting point).

Summary

- The subject of natural philosophy is mobile beings: i.e., things which have in themselves a principle of movement.
- We are seeking the principles, causes, and elements of natural things.
- A principle is *the first thing from which anything is or comes to be.*
- A cause is *that upon which something depends for its being or coming to be.*
- An element is *the first material cause of a thing which is indivisible with respect to its form.*

CHAPTER 3

The Method to Follow in Natural Philosophy

The Three Roads in Human Knowledge

Recall from our logic course that whenever we come to know something new, we must begin from what is better known to us in order to come to know what is less well known. This order of before and after in our knowledge[8] is sometimes called a road or path in our knowledge because, when we walk down a road, we proceed in an order from what is before to what comes after. The English word *method* comes from the Greek word *methodos* which means "over a road" (Greek: *meta hodos*). Hence, when we are seeking the right method to follow, we are actually looking for the right road to travel over in our knowledge, the right order to follow from what comes before in our knowledge to what comes after.

It turns out that there are three such roads in human knowing, based upon the three ways in which things can be better known to us. These three roads can be called the natural road, the common road, and the private road. Let's look at each one separately.

[8] Remember the chapter from the *Categories* on "before and after," in which the third sense of before and after was before and after in our knowledge.

The *natural road* is the order in human knowing that comes from the fact that all of our knowledge begins in the senses. Men have both sense knowledge and intellectual (or rational) knowledge. But human knowledge begins in the senses and then enters into the reason. This order in our knowledge from the senses into reason is what we call the natural road. Therefore, we find that sensible things are better known to us than understandable things. For example, we know the sensible experience of motion before we understand what motion is. And since sensible things are typically effects of causes, according to the natural road, we will move from effect to cause.

A second road is called the *common road* because it is an order that must be followed commonly in every kind of rational knowledge. This road is not between the senses and reason, but rather, once things have come to be known in reason, this is a road followed in reason itself from the better known to the lesser known. This common road is what we discover in logic, since logic is the art of coming to know what we do not know from what we do know. For example, in every science, premises must come before conclusions. And in every science, we must define before we demonstrate. Moreover, in making definitions, the genus is known before the specific differences are, etc.

A third road is called the *private road*, since it is an order to be followed in acquiring some particular science, like geometry or physics. This road is private to that one science, and is determined by the subject matter of that science. Each subject reveals itself in a way peculiar to it, so the method of coming to know that subject will also be peculiar to it in some way. For example, fruit trees are known by means of the kind of fruit they bear, so we begin studying them by examining their fruit. In fact, the private road is really many different roads, since there are as many private roads as there are different sciences. Thus, for example, in mathematics, we generally move from the simple to the complex, from the elements to the composed (e.g., lines to surfaces), and from cause to effect. In theology, we begin with God and then move on to consider creatures. In natural philosophy, we begin with the confused whole and move to the more elementary parts, etc.

These three roads are not completely independent orders in human knowing. They stand in a definite relationship to one another. The natural road comes first and is presupposed to all of our knowledge. The common road comes next. Finally, once we have traveled down the natural and common roads, we can begin to follow the road private to the particular field of study in which we are interested. In this chapter, we are seeking to discover the road private to natural philosophy.

The Order of Coming to Know the Principles, Causes, and Elements of Natural Things[9]

Assuming that natural things do have principles, causes, and elements, where should we begin in order to look for them and find them? The general answer comes from our study of logic: we should always begin from what is better known to us. But what is better known to us in the realm of natural things? A text from Aristotle will be very helpful here.

> The natural path is to go from the things which are more known and certain to us toward things which are more certain and knowable by nature. For the more known to us and the simply knowable are not the same. Whence it is necessary to proceed in this way from what is less certain by nature but more certain to us, toward what is more certain and more knowable by nature. But the things which are at first obvious and certain to us are rather confused, and

[9] Supplementary text: St. Thomas, *Commentary on the Physics*, I.1, n. 5-11.

> from these the elements and principles become known later by dividing them [out]. Whence it is necessary to go from the universal to the particulars.
>
> For the whole is more known according to sensation, and the universal is a certain whole. For the universal embraces many things within it as parts.
>
> In a way, the same thing happens in the relation of a name to its account. For the name signifies indistinctly some whole, as "circle" [does], but the definition of [circle] divides into the single parts.
>
> And children at first call all men "fathers" and all women "mothers," but later they distinguish each of them.[10]

Aristotle here refers to the natural road or the natural path.[11] He notes that things that are better known to us are not more knowable in themselves. That is, there is less reality in them, and less to be known about them. For example, the statement "the whole is greater than the part" is very well known to us, but there is not much information there. It is a very vague and general statement. On the other hand, the statement "God contains the perfections of all things" is something not well known to us, but it is full of meaning and contains a great deal of information. So we tend to know the least profound truths and the least intelligible things before we know more profound truths and more intelligible things.

---

[10] Aristotle, *Physics*, Bk. I, ch. 1.

[11] This path is called natural not because it is the natural road from senses into reason described above, but because it is the road appropriate to follow in studying natural things. The natural road from the senses into reason is called 'natural' because it is an order determined by human nature, which has both sense and rational knowledge. The road for natural philosophy is called 'natural' because it follows the order in coming to know natural things, like trees and rocks.

The next point Aristotle makes is that the things that are better known to us tend to be more general and universal, and less distinct. And he gives three different examples of different kinds of wholes and parts to illustrate how that happens in human knowledge. First, he gives the example of the sensible, integral whole. (Remember that the integral whole is composed of its parts so as to be the sum of its parts.) When we see a cow, for example, we see the whole cow before we distinctly see and discriminate its parts, such as its hooves and horns and eyelashes, or even more particularly, its cells or molecules. As we inspect the cow more closely, we begin to see those other, smaller parts, but only after we have seen the whole.

Second, he gives the example of the understandable integral whole (sometimes called a formal integral whole). For a circle is at first understood in a general way, but after some thought the parts of the definition of circle become apparent, until we have a distinct understanding of circle as a closed figure in which all the points on the boundary line are equidistant from a center point. You would have noticed this in the chapter on definition from last quarter's logic class: first, you have a general sense of the meaning of the name you use (which is clear since you use the name correctly when you speak). Later, after some thought, the parts or elements of the definitions of those names become apparent.

Finally, Aristotle gives an example of a sensible thing which is more universal. For when a child knows his father, he knows him not as the man who generated him, but rather simply as his first sensible experience of man. Hence, he attributes the name "father" to the thing he knows as man. So he knows the whole "man" before he knows the particular kind of man "father."

This order to follow in natural philosophy is very important, since it shows us that we should look for principles on a more universal level before we look for principles and causes which are more specific. Thus, for example, we should look for principles responsible for the changes observed in all natural things before we look for the principles specifically responsible for the growth of a tree or the flight of a bird.

Summary

- A road in human knowledge is an order we follow from the better known to the lesser known.
- There are three such roads: one natural, one common, and one private to each science.
- The road private to natural philosophy requires that the principles and causes of the most universal aspects of natural things should be sought first.

CHAPTER 4

Is Motion Even Possible?

Before beginning our investigation into what are the general principles and causes of natural things, we first need to consider an objection: is motion even possible?

This objection may at first seem to be unnecessary, or even silly. After all, it is apparent to the senses that motion exists. Just wave your hand in front of your face if you think you need proof. True and certain as this is, the fact remains that many of the most intelligent philosophers of the past have struggled with this problem. And while our initial certitude of the existence of motion will remain unshaken in the face of any arguments to the contrary, nevertheless, it will be helpful to consider these arguments in order to understand the nature and characteristics of motion better.

Here are some of the arguments that some of the most intelligent philosophers have wrestled with.

First, it seems that motion and coming to be cannot exist. For nothing comes to be from nothing. If something came to be from nothing, then that from which it came to be would at least have to be a principle of something, which would mean that it wasn't "nothing" after all.

On the other hand, nothing can come to be from what already exists either. For if what comes to be is identical in every way with the being from which it came to be, then there would be no coming to be, but the same thing would simply remain what it was, completely changeless.

Yet, if what comes to be is different in any way from that being from which it comes to be, then what is the source of this difference? It cannot be that the difference comes from the original being, since it does not already possess this difference. And nothing gives what it does not have. Hence, the only explanation for this difference is that the difference came from nothing. But we already saw that nothing comes from nothing. Therefore, if nothing comes from nothing, and nothing comes from what already exists, it follows that nothing at all comes to be: i.e., there is no motion or coming to be. This argument is that which was given by Parmenides.

Here is a second argument taken from Zeno's famous paradoxes. In order for something to move from one place to another place, it will first have to get halfway to that place. But in order to get to the half-way point, it will have to go halfway there too. But this will go on to infinity. And since you cannot cross over an infinity of places, there is no way to move from one place to another place. Nor does it matter how fast you go, for it is impossible to count up to infinity, no matter how fast you count. Therefore, motion is impossible. Take some time to discuss these arguments in class.[12] What is true in all of these? Are there any equivocal terms? Do these arguments follow proper logical argumentation?

---

[12] Notice the similarity between Parmenides's argument that there can be no coming to be and Socrates's argument in the *Meno* that there can be no coming to know. Socrates had said: you cannot come to know from what you don't know, since how would you recognize it when you found it. You cannot come to know from what you already know, since then you haven't learned anything at all, you simply always knew it. Therefore, there is no coming to know (i.e., learning).

Now that you've discussed them, let's see what the solution should be. Analyzing the first argument, we see that it is an either-or argument in this form:

X comes from either A or B.

X does not come from A.

X does not come from B.

Therefore, X does not come to be.

X stands for "being." A stands for "non-being." B stands for "being." The conclusion is: being does not come to be. Or, put another way: there is no coming to be, there is no motion.

The first thing we must do to address this argument is to go back to our fundamental certitude from our senses that there is motion. Remember that at the beginning of the year we saw that philosophy is an account of the universal causes of reality. Philosophy must therefore explain our experiences, not explain them away or give a replacement for our experiences of the real world. Consequently, any explanation of reality that does away with the existence of motion is not a good explanation of reality. Even if someone were to assert that there is only the appearance of motion, this appearance of motion would still be a kind of motion. Motion is the given, not something up for debate.

Therefore, it is obvious that one of the premises in the argument must be false. Look at the three premises again:

1. Being does not come from non-being;

2. Being does not come from being (i.e., from itself); and

3. Being comes from either being or non-being.

All of these seem to be true. What could be the source of the error?

Recall from our logic class that often, one of the sources of error in arguments is equivocation: using a word in two different senses in the same argument. The word "being" is certainly a word that has several meanings. Let's use the second tool of dialectic to distinguish some of the meanings of the word "being," or "is."

Consider the following scenario. A man is in a fight with another man. The first man pulls out a loaded gun and is about to shoot. We often say, even before a shot is fired: that man (the one without the gun) *is* dead. At the same time, we might also say: that man *is* not dead yet. We admit that both statements are true, even though opposite predicates are asserted of the same subject. What is the difference between these two statements? In the first statement *is* means "is about to be" while in the second statement *is* means "is actually."

Something similar happens with regard to the premises of Parmenides's argument. The statement "being does not come from being" is true if "being" means "what actually is" or "what already is" in both cases. But if the second time "being" is used it means "what is able to be" or "what is about to be," then this statement is false. It is false to say that what actually is does not come from what is able to be. Hence, we arrive at distinctions of enormous importance that give us the answer to our dilemma. If we distinguish between 1) actual being, 2) ability to be, and 3) non-being, we can see that the argument no longer follows. The second kind of being, ability to be, we call "potential being," as opposed to "actual being" or simple "non-being." Another way of seeing the fallacy in Parmenides's argument is to consider the either-or statement: either being comes from (actual) being or being comes from (pure) non-being. This statement does not give an exhaustive division since being might come from potential being, which is in between actual being and pure non-being.

This distinction between actual being and potential being also resolves the paradox of Zeno. While it *is impossible* to pass successively over an *actually* infinite number of places, it *is not impossible* to pass over a distance which is only *potentially* divisible into an infinite number of places. For that distance is actually finite and only potentially infinite. This is helpful for seeing what motion is: it is not an infinite succession of beings in place, just as a line or distance is not composed from an actually infinite number of points. When something moves from one place to another, the moving thing is not actually *in* any of the places in between (unless it comes to a stop at one of the intermediate places). The mobile (the thing which is movable) passes through each place, but is never actually *in* the intermediate places precisely because it is in motion and not at rest *in* a place. It is only able to be in those places in the event that the mobile is brought to rest.

This analysis of the arguments against the possibility of motion is helpful in many ways. First, it brings to light the very important philosophical distinction between actual and potential being.[13] Second, this analysis manifests that the ultimate basis for making judgments about the truth of a conclusion in natural philosophy is that these conclusions must conform to our basic sense experiences. Philosophers will sometimes express this by saying that natural philosophy resolves to sensation: that is, the foundational experiences which natural philosophy has to explain, and not explain away, are sense experiences. In a similar way, mathematics resolves to imagination, and logic resolves to intellect.

13 Sometimes I will refer to this distinction in various ways: being in act vs. being in ability; actual being vs. potential being; being in act vs. being in power; actual being vs. virtual being. These are all nuanced versions of the same fundamental distinction.

Summary

- Because motion is a difficult concept to grasp, there are many difficulties which arise in trying to understand motion.
- Apparent contradictions are just that: apparent. The philosopher can never accept an account of reality that involves a real contradiction.
- The distinction between actual and potential being resolves the apparent contradiction about motion.
- The ultimate basis for our judgments in natural philosophy is our sense experience. Any account of the natural world which is opposed to our sense experience is an incorrect account and must be changed.

CHAPTER 5

The Principles of Change in All Natural Things

The Three Principles of Change in All Natural Things

We have seen that natural philosophy considers things which have an intrinsic source of motion. We have also seen that the principles and causes of natural things which we ought to look for first are those responsible for the most universal aspects of natural things. Therefore, since motion is common to all natural things, let us begin by seeking the principles which must be involved in every motion.

Whenever one thing changes into another thing, we notice the same principles at work. Let's take a simple example. A carpenter takes a desk and changes it into a bed, as represented in the diagram below:

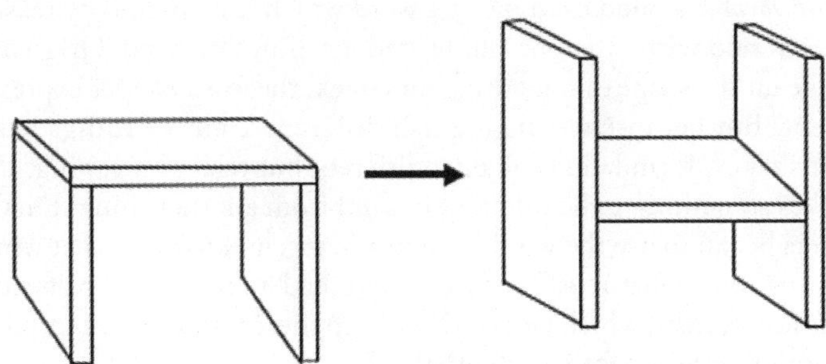

In this transformation, we see that something has changed, while something else has remained the same. The shape has changed, but the same wood was used in both the desk and the bed. This is not only true for the bed and the desk, but for any number of things which are transformed into one another. For example, when wax is reshaped from a ball to a cube, the matter stays the same while the form changes. When an apple ripens from green to red, the subject matter (the apple skin) stays the same, while the form (in this case the color or sweetness) changes. When a cow eats grass, the matter of the grass is transformed into the form of the cow. Thus, we could say very generically, whenever one thing changes into another, the matter remains through the change while the form is different. Notice here that form means more than just shape.[14] In this context, it means whatever it is that makes one thing different in kind from another (e.g., the shape, the color, the kind of thing it is, even a thing's place). So we can identify already two principles involved in every motion or change: matter and form.

But someone might ask: why does the matter have to remain the same throughout a change from one thing into another? Couldn't both the matter and the form change? Well, yes, both the matter and the form of a thing might cease to be, and a new matter and a new form come to be. But this would be the annihilation of one

---

[14] The word *form* is a good example of a word which is equivocal by reason: a name that is said with different, but related meanings in mind. Originally, form just meant the shape of something; in Greek, the word *morphe* expresses this concept. But because we distinguish different kinds of things based upon their shapes, form later took on a different but related meaning: that which makes something to be different in kind from another thing. Finally, philosophers began to use the word form in a new sense, namely: that which makes a thing to be what it is. The Greeks also had a different word for this different concept, *eidos*, which helped them keep these two similar but subtly different notions distinct from each other.

thing and the creation of a completely different thing, so that it would be incorrect to say that the first thing changed into the second thing. Rather, the first thing ceased to be, and the second thing came to be, without any real relationship between them. Therefore, in every case where one thing changes into another thing, the matter must remain throughout the change.

So far so good. Matter is what remains through a change, and form is what is different that makes the matter to be a new kind of thing. But there is one other detail we have missed. There is one additional thing necessary for one thing to change into another thing: the original form has to be different from the final form. If I start off with a bed and end up with a bed of exactly the same shape, would I say that the bed changed? No. I need to start with something that's not a bed to begin with. So there is a third element involved in every coming to be: the thing which is changed must lack the final form into which it is about to be changed. A simple way of expressing this third principle is to call it *privation*: that is, the lack of the final form. In the above example, the privation is the "lack of the form of bed." Notice that the privation is correctly expressed as "the lack of the form of bed." It would not be correct to refer to the privation as "the form of desk" since privation is not something positive. In fact, it does not matter whether at the beginning of the transformation it has the form of desk or some other form. What matters is only that it *lacks* the form of bed.

In summary, we can say that three principles are involved in every change: matter, form, and privation. These are defined as follows: Matter is *that out of which something comes and remains in it*. Privation is *that out of which something comes but does not remain in it*. Form is *that which makes a thing to be what it is*. Notice further how form and privation are opposed to each other as having to lacking, and even in a way like contraries. This harmonizes with the findings of the early natural philosophers who all in some way identified the principles of coming to be as three. For example, Thales had water (matter), density (form), and rarity (privation). Empedocles had the four elements (matter), love (form), and strife (privation).

Notice also that there is a certain likeness between matter and privation, since they have the same genus of their definition. So don't confuse them. Plato, for example, confused matter with privation for this reason.

Per Se and *Per Accidens* Principles

When we say that matter, form, and privation are the three principles of every coming to be, do we mean that they are all principles in the same way? No. Which of the three seems different than the others? Privation is different, since it does not cause the change in itself, but rather is a precondition that happens to make the change possible. The lack of the form of bed is not some real, positive being in things, but rather it is a condition that our reason notices must exist for change to take place. Therefore, we say that matter and form are *per se* principles, since they cause change through or by themselves, whereas privation is a *per accidens* principle, since it happens to be necessary as a precondition for every change.

Summary

- Matter is *that from which something comes and remains in it.*
- Privation is *that from which something comes and does not remain in it.*
- Form is *that which makes a thing to be what it is.*
- Matter and form are *per se* principles of change, while privation is a *per accidens* principle of change.

CHAPTER 6

Substantial Change, Substantial Form, and Prime Matter

Substance and Substantial Changes

So far we have talked about matter, form, and change in general terms, using examples taken from man-made things, like the bed and the desk above. The reason this is helpful is that man-made things are very well known to us. We are their causes, and we are responsible for the changes they undergo. But an analysis of change only based upon man-made things is insufficient to understand the changes that happen in the natural world, since natural things are not man-made. Indeed, the artificial is in some way opposed to the natural.

To understand natural changes better, let's return to a distinction we saw already in logic: the distinction between substance and accident. In logic, we defined first substance (or individual substance) as that which is neither said of, nor present in, another thing. On the other hand, an accident is necessarily present in another thing. For example, this dog, Fido, is an individual substance, and brown is an accident, since brown is present in Fido, but Fido isn't present in or said of anything else. This way of distinguishing substances from accidents is appropriate for logic, because the logician is especially interested in the differences between things that are reflected in our way of speaking about them. But the natural philosopher is not so much interested in the ways we speak about things as in the very manner in which they exist in themselves. So we can give another definition of substance and accident that is more in keeping with the way a natural philosopher considers reality. Substance is that which exists by itself or on its own (*per se*), while accidents are those beings which exist only in or through another thing (*per aliud*). Notice that this is not opposed to the way the logician defined substance and accident, it is just a way of defining which emphasizes the way substances and accidents exist in themselves.

Now that we have a better understanding of the difference between substance and accident, we can distinguish between substantial and accidental changes. A substantial change happens when one substance changes into another substance. For example, when a cow eats grass, the substance of grass is changed into the substance of a cow. An accidental change happens when a substance goes from having one accident to another accident. For example, when clay goes from having the shape of a sphere to having the shape of a cube, the same substance, clay, has now one accident (the shape of a sphere), now another accident (the shape of a cube). As you may have already guessed, accidental changes can happen in any one of the nine categories of accidents: quantity, quality, relation, acting upon, undergoing, position, where, when, and outfit. So, for example, going from green to red is an accidental change in an apple. Going from sitting to standing is an accidental change in a man, etc.

Is Substantial Change Possible?

A difficulty arises when we try to understand exactly how substantial changes take place. Take our healthy, brown, grass-eating, bovine friend. What happens when she eats the grass at her feet? Well, the grass gets changed into cow of course. But how? What is the matter which remains throughout the change from grass to cow? If the matter which remains through the change is the grass itself, then how now brown cow? Put another way, if the grass remains through the change, then the grass must still be there at the end, and so the cow will simply be made out of grass. Most people, I think, would say that the grass is itself made out of some more fundamental element or matter, like carbon and hydrogen, or like protons and neutrons, or quarks,[15] or whatever you think is the ultimate element out of which things are made. These elements are in the grass at the beginning, and are in the cow at the end. But when the cow eats the grass, these elements get rearranged into cow protein molecules and cells, etc.

But here is the difficulty: according to this account, the same actual substance is present in both the grass and the cow, but is merely rearranged. So there hasn't been a substantial change after all, but only an accidental change. The same substance changed its shape, position, or some other accidental feature. At the beginning and at the end, what we really have is a rearranged heap of quarks. Another difficulty is this: is a cow one substance or many substances? The same thing cannot be one substance and many substances, because a substance is that which exists on its own, what simply speaking *is*. Simply speaking, the same thing can't be quarks and a cow at the same time. So I can't have it both ways: I can't say that a cow is one substance and the molecules or quarks (or whatever) of the cow are many substances. The same

[15] A quark is the most recently postulated "ultimate particle" out of which all other particles (protons, neutrons, electrons, etc.) are made. We simply refer to them for the sake of convenience as if they were the ultimate substance out of which things are made, without pretending to make a judgment about the truth of the theory of quarks.

thing cannot be many and one at the same time in the same way. If the material making up the cow is itself many actual substances, then a cow is more or less a complicated machine, a sophisticated robot, which has only an accidental unity, not a substantial unity: a cow would not be one substance simply speaking. The difficulty is even more apparent when we reflect upon our own experience of ourselves as substances. We do not experience ourselves as many things, but as one thing having many parts.

Yet it is undeniable that we are somehow composed of other substances. If I go for a run, I begin to perspire. The drops that fall to the ground are substances made up of water and salt, among other things. They are clearly not the same substance as I am after they have separated from my body. Why should I think that, when this water and salt are in me before I begin to perspire, they are one substance with me? The same can be said for any number of things that go from being a part of my body to existing on their own apart from me. We seem to have tied a knot that has us caught in a contradiction: we seem to be both one substance and many substances.

Fortunately, we have been in a conundrum like this before. And good philosophers know that when faced with an apparent contradiction, there is always some distinction that will deepen our understanding of things and get us out of the contradiction. Let's go back to the apparent contradiction we faced earlier in this book: being cannot come from being and being cannot come from non-being. We resolved this contradiction by a deeper understanding of the term "being," and we distinguished between actual being and potential being, where potential being is in some way between actual being and non-being. Can we make use of the same or a similar distinction here?

While we cannot say that the same thing is actually one substance and actually many substances at the same time, we can say that the same thing is actually one substance and *potentially* many substances at the same time. Let's take an interesting example: if you take an ordinary earthworm and cut it in half, both halves will heal and become whole worms again. Does that mean there were actually two worms there all along? No, but there were potentially two worms there, and the division made that potency, that ability, into an actuality.[16] In the same way, a human being, a cow, or any other living organism is able to be divided into many different substances. But those substances exist only potentially, or in ability, so long as they are present within the living organism. Once they are separated out, by whatever means, they become actual substances existing on their own.[17]

We can refine this understanding of many substances existing potentially in a single, actual substance by noticing that, even when they exist only potentially, certain characteristics or traits of the many substances within a single actual substance remain. For example, the weight of the molecules of a cow when they exist apart from the cow is the same as the weight of those very molecules when they form part of the cow's substance. Whenever

---

[16] By the way, that is how identical twins form in the womb. At an early stage of cell division, one of the cells breaks from the others and begins to develop all by itself into an independent and complete human being.

[17] Sometimes the reverse process can occur, as in an organ transplant. The organ, when it is first introduced into the new body, is not part of that body's substance, but gradually gets assimilated into its substance so that eventually it becomes part of the substance of the recipient. Precisely because it is not part of the body's substance at the beginning is why organ transplant failure is not uncommon: the body rejects it as a part of its substantial unity and treats it as something foreign to be destroyed. The same does not happen with matter that is not able to be assimilated by the body. For example, a gold filling in a tooth always remains a distinct substance in the recipient.

a substance is present potentially in another substance in such a way as to preserve some of its characteristics or traits, we say that this substance exists virtually (or "in power," from the Latin word *virtus*, meaning "power"). "Virtual" and "potential" mean nearly the same thing, but virtual adds the idea of an active ability or power, so that a substance existing virtually in another substance seems to be "almost" actual. Nevertheless, to exist virtually is not the same as existing actually. It is still only potential existence.

What Is Substantial Form?

Now that we have seen that substantial change is possible, and we have also seen that every change involves going from one form to another, the next question that naturally comes to mind is: what do we mean by "form" when we say one substance changes into another substance?

Recall that all we mean by form in this context is "whatever makes a thing to be what it is." What makes a square to be a square? Its shape, its form. But when we say that a substance has a form, we are not referring to what makes the substance to be in some accidental way, like its shape (indeed, your shape can change quite dramatically, yet you remain the same substance you have always been). Rather, when we say that a substance has a form, we mean *that which makes a substance to be what it is simply speaking, or essentially*: whatever makes a man to be a man, whatever makes a dog to be a dog, is its substantial form.

Because it is difficult to know the definitions of most natural substances, many have come to the conclusion that there is really no such thing as substantial form. That is, there is no such thing as a cause which makes a substance to be essentially what it is and essentially one thing.

Aristotle was the first philosopher to see clearly the reality of substantial form through the analogy of accidental forms. Accidental forms, such as the shape of a statue or the color of a rose, are better known to us, since they are immediately evident to the senses, while substantial forms can only be known by the mind (recall the natural road from the senses into reason). Aristotle reasoned that it is evident to the mind that certain things like animals or plants are substantially one, and have their own unique form that makes them to be what they are. Although such things are composed of many parts, like flesh and blood and cells, these parts do not actually exist as independent substances within the whole, but only potentially as parts, or virtually as parts, since many of the characteristics of these parts still remain (like their weight or their chemical properties, etc.).[18]

However, as we said above, many have rejected this insight of Aristotle and claim instead that the unity of wholes, such as animals and plants and chemical compounds, can simply be explained as an accidental unity, that is, an arrangement of actually distinct substances, much like the unity of an artifact such as an automobile or a machine.

There are many obvious facts which are opposed to this position. We do not propose these facts as strict demonstrations or proofs that there are many different kinds of substances and corresponding substantial forms. Rather we take it as self-evident that many substances exist. However, we can use dialectic arguments to help manifest that this statement is self-evident.

First of all, our inward experience of ourselves as one thing is the first and best knowledge we have of substance. When we say that something is one substance, this is said by reference to our

[18] See St. Thomas Aquinas, *Summa Theologiae*, Ia, q.76, a.4, ad.4.

own experience of substantial unity. Our substantial unity is the primary analogate for the substantial unity we observe in other things. It is our awareness of our inner operations (for example, our sensations, thoughts, and emotions), which makes us aware of our substantial unity. When we see with our eyes, we do not experience two acts of seeing: that of our eyes and that of ourselves. We experience ourselves, our substance, as the one thing that sees. When a part of an ordered whole, like an army, acts, it is more properly the individual part which acts, and only in a secondary or metaphorical way that the whole army acts. When a soldier pulls the trigger of his gun, we attribute that act to the individual soldier, and if we were to say that the army pulled the trigger, we would only be speaking metaphorically, not properly. It is the reverse with the parts of a being having substantial unity. It is more proper to say that I saw the movie last night than to say my eyes saw the movie last night. Perhaps the most forceful evidence that you are one substance comes from the fact that you experience yourself as the single, ultimate subject of your own knowledge. What would it mean to say that you know or think that you are many substances? If you were not one substance, then you could never claim to know anything, since there is no "you" who knows. The subject of your knowledge is not a "we" or a "those," but an "I."

We observe the same thing in other persons and animals. For it is impossible that sensation be found in a subject which is not *per se* (substantially) one. For if a sensing being were only accidentally one being, then there would have to be as many sensations as parts which sense. For example, if an arm were not one substance with the rest of its body, then we could say that the arm felt pain, but not the whole animal. Yet this is contrary to our experience. Therefore, whatever has sensation must be admitted to have a substantial form.

Are there substantial forms of non-living, non-sensing beings? For the sake of argument, let us assume that every substance is made up of other, smaller substances which are its parts. It follows that these parts are themselves composed of other smaller substances, and so on to infinity. Now since there cannot be an infinite regress of material causes, there must exist some first part, some ultimate particle which is itself not composed of other substances. And since this first indivisible part has no parts of its own, it cannot have an accidental unity, but must rather have a substantial unity. But if it must be allowed that this lowest being in nature has a substantial form, then why in principle should substantial forms be denied of higher substances? This position is even more unreasonable given the fact that human beings have a substantial unity. For in that case, the highest being in nature and the lowest being in nature necessarily have substantial forms, but nothing in between is allowed to have a substantial form.

Another way it can be shown that non-living things have their own substantial forms is to see the way in which they act when combined with one another. In certain chemical compounds, two substances unite in such a way that the properties of the whole are contrary to the properties of the parts, as when hydrogen and oxygen unite to form water. Both hydrogen and oxygen feed fire, but water extinguishes fire. This is a sure indication that there is not just a pile of hydrogen and oxygen which are closer together when water is formed, but that water is an entirely new substance from either hydrogen or oxygen.

So these are some arguments that can help show that, in the natural world, there are in fact many substances, each of which has a form that makes it to be *that* substance and no other.

Prime Matter

But if, as we have seen, there is such a thing as substantial form, and every form is the form of some kind of matter, it follows that there will be a matter in which these substantial forms are found. Let us call the matter which underlies all substantial forms "prime matter," since it is the first matter out of which all substances are made. In what kind of matter will we find substantial forms? The first temptation is to imagine or think of prime matter as some kind of gelatinous substance, some colorless, shapeless slime. But this would simply be to make prime matter itself into an actual substance, amorphous as it may seem, and this pushes the question back further: What is the matter of the substance which we call prime matter?

The notion of prime matter is a slippery notion, and very hard to grasp. So let's begin with something easy to grasp about prime matter. Let's give as a kind of nominal definition of prime matter *whatever remains throughout a substantial change*. Remember that whenever one substance changes into another substance, something must remain through the change—otherwise, the first substance is merely annihilated and the second substance created, so the one does not change into the other. But we very clearly experience substances changing into one another, like the grass changing into the cow, or the eggs you had for breakfast changing into you. Something must have remained through the change, so given our nominal definition of prime matter, it is clear that the thing we are naming "prime matter" corresponds to some existing thing.

But what is the essential nature of this thing that remains throughout the substantial change? Is it a substance or not? Let's construct an either-or argument to see if we can't get at the nature of prime matter. Either prime matter is a substance or not a substance. And if it is not a substance, then it is either an accident or nothing at all. Are these the only options? Have we made an exhaustive division? Think carefully. We can also distinguish substance into what is actually a substance or potentially a substance. So that leaves us with four possibilities: prime matter is either an actual substance, a potential substance, an accident, or nothing at all. Let's use this division to construct our either-or argument as follows:

Prime matter is that which remains through a substantial change from a first substance to a second substance.

That which remains though a substantial change is either:

a. actually a substance,

b. potentially a substance,

c. an accident, or

d. nothing at all.

But *d* is false, since if nothing at all remains then the first substance did not change into the second substance.

And *c* is false, since accidents depend upon substances, not vice versa. So if there is a new substance, there must be new accidents.

And *a* is false, since if prime matter is actually a substance, then one substance will actually be two substances. For:

> Either prime matter is:
>
> the same as the first substance;
>
> or the same as the second substance;
>
> or different from the first and second substance.

> But if prime matter is the same as the first substance, then since prime matter remains through the change, it will still be there with the second substance, so at the end of the change the second substance will be two substances.
>
> And if prime matter is the same as the second substance, then it was also there at the beginning of the change, so the first substance will be two substances.
>
> And if prime matter is neither the first or second substance, then both at the beginning of the change and at the end of it, one substance will be two substances.

Therefore, since *a*, *c*, and *d* are false, *b* is true, namely, prime matter is only potentially a substance, but is not actually a substance.

And so we have reasoned to the nature of prime matter. Prime matter is that which is only able to be a substance. It is pure potency in the category of substance. This is a difficult concept to grasp, since we cannot imagine pure potency, but we can understand that it must be true by reasoning from what we do know for certain from our experience. We know that there are many kinds of substances. We know that substantial change takes place. And we know that one substance cannot actually be many substances at the same time. Based upon these facts of our experience, we must conclude that there is a matter underlying substantial change, and this prime matter is only potentially a substance.

For the sake of trying to grasp the concept of prime matter a little better, we can use an analogy to things that are better known.

Shape : wood :: substantial form : prime matter

This analogy helps us to understand a little better what prime matter is. But every analogy limps. That is, every analogy is in some way imperfect (since then it would be exactly the same case if there were no difference). So too in this case, since the wood gives existence to the accidents in it, including shape. But substantial form is what gives existence to prime matter, or vice versa.

Summary

- Substantial change is *the change of one substance into another.*
- There are many natural kinds of substances and hence many substantial forms.
- A substance is composed of substantial form and prime matter, where substantial form means "*that which makes a substance to be what it is simply speaking*" and prime matter is that which remains throughout the substantial change.
- Prime matter can be defined more essentially as "*pure potency in the category of substance.*"
- Because prime matter is not actually a substance, but only potentially, it cannot be known directly, but only through analogy.

CHAPTER 7

The Definition of Nature

What Is Nature and What Kinds of Things Are Natural?[19]

Now that we have seen in a general way the principles of all natural things, we are in a better position to arrive at a more refined definition of nature. Recall that we originally approached the idea of nature by contrasting nature with art, and natural things with artificial things. From this contrast we saw more clearly that natural things are those which have within themselves a source or principle of motion. And we have seen from the last chapter that both form and matter are intrinsic principles of the motion of natural things. So let's see if we can arrive at a more distinct definition of nature from what we already know.

First, we should observe that the word "nature" has several related meanings. It is a word which is equivocal by reason.[20] We want to focus on the sense of nature which is *the intrinsic principle of motion in natural things*: that which is responsible for their coming to be, their movement, their growth, their development, their perfection. The first thing that we should observe is that things not only move on account of their nature, but they also rest. A rock naturally moves downward, but it also naturally rests there once it has reached the lowest place. A boy

[19] Supplementary text: Ralph McInerny, *A First Glance at St. Thomas*, ch. 8.
[20] Supplementary text: Aristotle, *Metaphysics* Bk. V, ch. 4.

naturally grows into a man, but he also naturally remains a man once he has reached this term of growth. So we can immediately refine our definition of nature by saying nature is *an intrinsic principle of motion and rest.*

But do we call any intrinsic principle of motion and rest the nature of a thing? Take the following example: a man is walking, trips, and falls to the ground. He gets back up, complains a bit, then keeps on walking. There are several motions described there: walking, falling, getting up, complaining. But which one is due precisely to human nature? The man falls insofar as he is heavy. That is *part* of human nature, but it is something he shares with rocks and other heavy bodies. The man walks and gets up insofar as he is an animal with the power of locomotion, that is, motion from one place to another. That's *part* of his nature too, but it's something he shares with many animals. Neither of those motions seems to reflect precisely his nature as a man, as a rational animal. On the other hand, when he complains, this is a motion that results from his nature as rational, and this belongs first of all to man as such: it is proper to human nature, and the ability for such a motion belongs to all men. If we had to say what is the precise nature of a thing, we would have to refine our definition to say: it is *an intrinsic principle of motion and rest which belongs first of all to that kind of being.*

So far so good. We may think we are done, but there is one last minor precision that could be made just to avoid a possible confusion. Take this example: a man is a doctor. This means he has acquired the knowledge of medicine, so that the art of medicine is in him. If it just so happens that he gets sick and heals himself using the art of medicine he has, then that art of medicine would be 1) intrinsic to him; 2) a principle of the motion of healing in him; 3) and it would belong first and properly to man, and to no other natural thing. So it seems that the art of medicine in the doctor could be called his nature. Now no one really thinks that the art of medicine in the doctor is his human nature. Nevertheless, we should add something to the definition to make this clear. So we add that nature is also something essential or *per se*. That is, nature necessarily belongs to a thing because of what it is—it does not just happen to be in a thing. Consequently, we can give a complete definition of nature as follows: nature is *an intrinsic principle of motion and rest which is first and per se*.[21]

Given this definition of nature, we can see clearly that both the matter and the substantial form of a thing can be called its nature. Both matter and form are intrinsic to natural things. They are both principles of the motion and rest of a natural thing (for example, falling is due to the matter of a rock, and flying is due to the substantial form of a bird). They both belong to a thing essentially. And they both belong first or properly to the things they are in. For the substantial form of a thing belongs only to things of that nature, since the substantial form makes a thing to be what it is. And even the matter is in a sense proper to a thing's nature, since not just any matter will suit any kind of thing. Trees can't be made of flesh and animals can't be made of wood. Nevertheless, it is clear that form seems to be more nature than matter, since the form of a thing clearly belongs first to that thing and to no other, but the matter in some way can be common to many things of different kinds or natures.

How Can Natural Things Be Known?

At this point, before diving head-first into a scientific investigation of natural things, I think it will be helpful to raise a preliminary objection: how is it possible to know natural things in a truly scientific way?

---

[21] Supplementary text: St. Thomas, *Commentary on the Physics*, Bk. II, lect. 1-2.

Recall from logic that in order to have science (perfect reasoned-out knowledge) of a thing, we must know its proper causes *and* the thing known must be necessary. But this last condition seems to be false about all natural things. For all natural things, as we have seen, have matter, and therefore are not necessary, but contingent: it is possible for them to be or not be. So scientific knowledge about them seems impossible. This is a difficulty with which Plato struggled: how can we have certainty about material things if by their very nature they change?

Aristotle, the greatest student of Plato, realized Plato's struggle, and provides us with two brief answers. The first is this: though natural things are contingent, not *everything* about them is contingent. For example, their forms are always the same. Throughout the life of a man, many things about him change, but throughout he is still a man, having the substantial form of a man. Not only that, when he dies, "what a man is" does not die. So the substantial forms of things are in some real way necessary, and it is these necessary aspects of natural things that can be known scientifically. Of course, this also means that part of every natural thing cannot be known scientifically as well: the part that is contingent and due to the matter in it. So natural things cannot be known completely and perfectly by us. We can know them scientifically (that is, through their causes and with necessity) as universals, but not as individuals.

The second observation Aristotle makes is that there are different kinds of necessity. One kind of necessity is absolute: given the cause, the effect must be. Given a triangle as my cause, the effect of interior angles equaling two right angles is necessary. But there is also something called hypothetical necessity. On the hypothesis that such and such an effect has taken place, then its cause must have also existed. So if there is an oak tree, there must have been an acorn. Notice that it doesn't work the opposite way in natural things: if there is an acorn, it does not follow that there will be an oak tree. That's contingent. Yet the converse really is necessary. So even among individual natural things, there is some way of finding necessity and a kind of scientific account about them.

Summary

- Nature is *an intrinsic principle of motion and rest which is first and* per se.
- Both form and matter are the nature of a thing, but form more than matter.
- Natural things can be known scientifically so long as they are considered universally.
- There is a kind of necessity in natural things, not absolute, but hypothetical.

CHAPTER 8

The Four Causes Used for Demonstration in Natural Philosophy

Natural Things, Like Artificial Things, Have Four Kinds of Causes[22]

So far we have identified the most general principles of natural things, and we have also seen more distinctly what nature means, and how it is possible for us to have true science about natural things. Next, we need to investigate the causes of natural things.

It will be helpful to return to our analogy with artificial things. Remember that art imitates nature, since art is an effect of the order within the human mind, while the order in the human mind ultimately is traced back to the order discovered in nature. For example, the order of parts put into an airplane is like the order of parts discovered in flying birds: wings for lift, an aerodynamic body for easily passing through the air, and a tail for stabilizing during flight. It is therefore likely that the kinds of causes responsible for artificial things are similar to the kinds of causes found in natural things.

Let's take an example of a simple artifact: a statue. What are the kinds of causes responsible for the coming to be and being of

[22] Supplementary texts: St. Thomas, Commentary on the Physics, Bk. II, lect. 5. And R. McInerny, *A First Glance at St. Thomas Aquinas*, ch. 9.

a statue of David? Well, first there has to be the material: marble. But the marble is not enough to explain why there is a statue of *David*, and not some other statue. Besides the marble, there must be some definite shape into which the marble is formed: this shape is the formal cause of the statue of David. So we have both material and formal causes responsible for the statue of David. But was the form always there? No. So how did it get there? By means of a sculptor. So we need to posit a further cause, some kind of moving cause that is responsible for the form coming to be in the matter. The matter by itself is indifferent to this form or that, so there must be some cause that determines the matter to have this form rather than that, David rather than, say, Goliath. We call this moving cause an agent cause. Agent cause is defined as *the first source of a thing's motion or coming to be*. So now, we have three causes responsible for the statue of David. But are these three enough to account fully for the statue? No. We would also have to ask the question: Why did the sculptor choose to sculpt the marble into this shape rather than that one? The sculptor would not sculpt unless he had some purpose in mind, some target or end or goal towards which he was aiming. This final kind of cause is called the end, or the final cause, since it is the final explanation for the thing which has been made or done. Why is there a statue of David? Because there is this marble in that shape. Why is the marble in that shape? Because the sculptor formed it that way. Why did the sculptor choose to form it that way? Because of the end he had in mind. That's the final explanation, that's the final cause you can give for the statue of David. Final cause can be defined as *that for the sake of which something is or comes to be*. The final cause is therefore a kind of good at which things aim: it is that which is perfective of another thing as its end or purpose. And this is exactly what we mean when we say something is good: it has fulfilled its purpose. The good and the final cause are equivalent.

Let's look at another example, just to make sure we have it down. What are the four causes of a knife? The four causes are: metal (material); a handle with a sharp blade (formal); some manufacturer or knife maker (agent); and its purpose to cut (final). So we have identified four kinds of causes in artificial things: material cause, formal cause, agent cause, and final cause. Moreover, we have seen that there is a definite order among all these causes. The matter is marble (or metal) because of the kind of form it is supposed to have. The form is introduced into the matter by the agent. And the agent acts for the sake of some end or purpose.

How do we know that every agent acts for an end? Because, unless there were some destination to determine the agent to one direction of motion rather than another, the agent would have no inclination to move at all.[23] Put another way, there is no such thing as motion in no direction. What about random motions, like when a child scribbles randomly on a piece of paper? Even there, what you really have is several different motions with several changes of direction. But each separate motion is in some direction.

Are all four also found in natural things? Well, we have already seen that material and formal causes are causes in all natural things. It is also obvious that there are causes of motion in nature as well (for example, what Empedocles called love and strife, or attractive and repulsive forces), so there must be agent causes in nature too. That leaves final cause.

[23] Supplementary text: St. Thomas, *Summa Theologiae*, I-IIae, q.1, a.2.

Do natural things exist or come into existence for the sake of some purpose or end?

In other words: does nature act for an end?

Final Causality in Nature: Discovered or Imposed?[24]

The *prima facie* (first face, or first appearance) evidence indicates that natural things do have purposes and that nature does act for an end. We think that it is good for the arctic hare to have all white fur to camouflage it from predators. We think that when an embryo grows and develops eyes, these eyes are for the sake of seeing, and that seeing is good for the animal that has sight. Not only that, but there seems to be a marvelous order and harmony among the various kinds of natural things. Plants seem to be for the sake of animals. And some animals seem to exist for the sake of others. Some animals even seem to build artifacts of their own, as if they were acting for some end. A bird builds its nest for the sake of having a home to lay its eggs and to rest at night. A spider weaves its web for the sake of catching prey. This *prima facie* evidence is so strong that even those who expressly deny that nature acts for an end can't help speaking as if nature acts for an end, even in the very books they have written to prove the opposite.[25]

But there are lingering questions and difficulties with this view. Aren't we anthropomorphizing (that's a big word that means: attributing properly human features to something non-human)? After all, we got this idea of final causality from art. It's not as obvious in nature. And let's face it, human beings have purposes because they are intelligent. Am I asking you to believe that all

[24] Supplementary text: Charles DeKoninck, *Lifeless World of Biology*.

[25] For example, Dr. W. S. Beck, in his book *Modern Science and the Nature of Life*, says, "The polar bear is white because white fur enhances his chances of survival. By going beyond what is observable, we have explained his color."

natural things are intelligent, that nature itself is intelligent? Perhaps nature only *looks like* it's acting for an end because we want it to, because we are imposing our way of thinking and causing on natural things. Maybe we could explain the appearance of acting for an end in nature by some other means so that we don't have to posit final cause as one of the causes in nature.

Evolution versus the Grand Design

It is precisely this line of reasoning that has led many thinkers to search for an explanation of the apparent purposefulness of nature and natural things in terms of causes that are blind and purposeless. Since purpose in nature is most obvious among living things, it is especially there that some alternative explanation has been sought. If you can show that there is no purpose among living things, animals and plants, then *a fortiori* (for even a better reason) purpose does not exist among non-living, natural things. By far the most widely accepted alternative explanation to the position that there is purpose in nature is the so-called theory of evolution. Most modern people think that this theory was first developed by a biologist named Charles Darwin in his work *On the Origin of Species*, in which he explained that blind (purposeless) causes like chance, necessity, and natural selection are sufficient to explain the diversity of natural life forms and the appearance of purpose among them. It is true that Darwin was the first to give a detailed account of the theory of evolution that fits with the detailed information we now have. However, as we shall later see, it was Empedocles, an ancient Greek philosopher, who first proposed that the appearance of purpose among living things was actually the result of purposeless causes. Although the records we have of his account are not as detailed and scientific as the account given by Darwin, all of the same principles—chance, necessity, and natural selection—were already posited by Empedocles more than two thousand years before Darwin wrote *On the Origin of Species.*

Regardless of who first proposed the theory of evolution, the question remains: is this alternative account such that we need no longer hold that there is purpose, final causality, in nature? Or does nature itself reveal a grand design and intelligence which is the ultimate and true explanation of the natural world?

Summary

- There are four kinds of causes: material, formal, agent, and final.
- All four kinds of causes are found in natural things, and the Natural Philosopher will demonstrate his conclusions using all four kinds of causes.
- Final causality is something really found in nature, not simply imposed by human thought.
- However, it is difficult to see how final cause can be in natural things, and many theories have attempted to explain the natural world without final cause.

CHAPTER 9

The Argument for Materialist Evolution

Making an Argument for Evolution

The purpose of this chapter is to lay out with as much clarity and forcefulness as possible the argument in favor of evolution as the result of purposeless causes. We call this the argument for "materialist" evolution, since in this argument, material cause is the primary cause invoked as the reason for evolution. We mentioned above that Empedocles is the first person recorded to have made this argument. Here is the argument as summarized by Saint Thomas:

> From the beginning of the formation of the world, the four elements were joined in the constitution of natural things, and thus the varied and many dispositions of natural things were produced. And in all those things, only that which happened to be suitable for some utility, as if it were made for that utility, was preserved. For such things had a disposition which made them suitable for being preserved, not because of some agent intending an end, but because of that which is *per se* vain, i.e., by chance. On the other hand,

> whatever did not have such a disposition was destroyed and is destroyed daily.[26]

This argument contains the fundamental principles behind the theory of evolution, even in its modern form. Changes happen by chance in living beings. Out of those chance mutations, be they big or small, some happen to be useful (even if a very small percentage). Hence, they end up being preserved and passed on. Since these useful living things predominate, in the end, it looks like nature intends to make things with purposes, when in fact, it just happened by chance without any intention.

Darwin's Argument

Charles Darwin amplified this argument and gave it forceful expression in his works. Here is a summary of his argument, together with a syllogistic breakdown of the argument:

All sensible things change. In particular we see that living beings grow into maturity, and that the offspring of most living beings varies in some way from the parents. Thus, it is clear that from generation to generation, it is possible that certain traits in the offspring of living beings will become more pronounced than others as some traits are reinforced and others are not. Now the primary way in which certain traits are reinforced is that the offspring which exhibit these traits survive to produce more like themselves, while others do not propagate in the same proportion. Now since all living beings are in competition for the same resources, it is clear that some will survive while others must perish for lack of resources. Thus, it is clear that those traits conducive to survival will become more pronounced, while those traits which are not conducive to survival will disappear. Those

[26] St. Thomas Aquinas, *Commentary on the Physics*, Bk. II, lect. 12.

beings which acquire these traits are called more perfect. In this manner, the conflict between the species results in the perfection of the surviving members. This is known as the "survival of the fittest," and the process by which the fittest predominate in the successive generations is called "natural selection."

Furthermore, among living beings we see a gradation from the simple to the more complex, and this gradation forms a sort of continuous chain from the simplest life forms up to man. Now it is reasonable to suppose that, due to the similarity of certain species (like man to chimpanzees), one has its origin in the other. Therefore, there is nothing to prevent us from supposing that the more perfect species is really a variation of the other which has come about over a period of time sufficient to allow for the gradual mutation of the less perfect species into the other. This process from the less perfect species to the more perfect species is known as evolution.

We must finally assert that this can be the only reasonable explanation of the development of complex life as we know it, since this explanation is at once self-sufficient and rests upon fewer principles to explain our experience. Thus, any explanation which requires that we posit a supreme being who guides this process is untenable, since this adds a superfluous principle which is in no way necessary to explain the observed facts. Therefore, we must hold that materialist evolution is the only acceptable explanation for the development of the species.

The following is a syllogistic breakdown of this argument:

1) All living beings change from generation to generation.
2) Some of those things which change <u>from generation to generation will change into something more fit for survival.</u>
3) Therefore, some living beings will change into something more fit for survival.

3) Some living beings will change into something more fit for survival.
4) That which is more fit for survival will survive more often than that which is less fit for survival.
5) Therefore, those living beings which change into something more fit for survival will survive more often than those less fit to survive.

5) Those living beings which change into something more fit for survival will survive more often than those less fit to survive.
6) That which survives more often is more perfect than that which survives less often.
7) Therefore, those living beings which change into something more fit for survival will become more perfect.

7) Living beings which are more fit for survival become more perfect.
8) What becomes more perfect eventually becomes so perfect that it will be different in kind.
9) Therefore, living beings which are more fit for survival eventually become more perfect kinds of living beings.

9) Living beings which are more fit for survival eventually become more perfect kinds of living beings.
10) To eventually become more perfect kinds of living beings is to develop eventually from the less perfect to the more perfect kind of living being.
11) Therefore, living beings eventually develop from less perfect kinds of living things into more perfect kinds of living beings.

11) Living beings eventually develop from less perfect kinds of living things into more perfect kinds of living beings.
12) The eventual development of living beings from the less perfect kind of living being to the more perfect kind is evolution.

    Therefore, living beings evolve.

Take time in class to evaluate the argument using the tools you learned in logic. In the next chapter we will provide a critique of this argument.

CHAPTER 10

Critiquing the Argument for Materialist Evolution

Once the argument in favor of materialist evolution has been set down in syllogistic form, it is much easier to see where there may be weaknesses in the argument.

There are some questions about the form of the argument. First of all, some of the premises are particular. Therefore, the conclusion must be understood to be particular, namely, that some living things evolve. The second difficulty concerning the form is with the first syllogism. The middle term, "things which change from generation to generation," is neither the subject of a universal premise, nor the predicate in a negative premise (SUN-PIN rule). So it seems that nothing follows. However, if one realizes that the first premise happens to be universally commensurate (since all things which have generations are living things, since only living things reproduce with distinct generations), then the first syllogism could be reformulated as a valid third figure syllogism.

Therefore, if there are remaining criticisms of the argument, they should be directed to one or more of the premises. After your discussion in class, it is likely that you identified two premises in particular as being doubtful. The first premise that seems false is "that which survives more often is more perfect than that which survives less often" (premise six in the syllogistic breakdown). The second premise which seems false is "what becomes more perfect eventually becomes so perfect that it will be different in kind" (premise eight in the syllogistic breakdown). Let's consider them one at a time.

Perfection is not the same as fitness for survival. One way this can be seen is that perfection seems to be an attribute intrinsic to a thing, while fitness for survival seems to be completely relative to external factors. A ninety-pound weakling is more fit to survive on a thin, plywood board over a shark tank than a fit, two-hundred-thirty-pound bodybuilder. The bodybuilder is physically more perfect, but his muscle mass is likely to cause the plywood board to break and turn him into shark-bait. Sponges are more fit to survive underwater than dogs, but that doesn't make dogs less perfect than sponges. Cockroaches are more fit to survive a nuclear holocaust than men, but that doesn't make cockroaches more perfect than men. So perfection is not identified with fitness for survival. Perfection seems to be something absolute by which things in the same genus can be compared. For example, we say that men are more perfect than the plants or other animals since, besides being able to grow and reproduce like plants, and besides having the various senses like the other animals, man also has reason, which is better than any sense (a sign of which is that a man would rather lose his sight or hearing than his mind). So we can say that the more perfect thing has everything that the less perfect thing has, and then something better additionally. The more perfect contains the less perfect and adds something else besides.

Notice also that a more perfect thing is better than a less perfect thing. For example, a man is better, has more goodness, than other animals. And animals are better than plants. This means that if we are to give a reason why some living things become more perfect, this reason will have to invoke final cause, since the final cause is the good of each thing, and explains why one thing is better than another. Put another way, the only way to prove that a living thing can become better or more perfect than another living thing would be through a cause which makes things to be better than others. And such a cause would have to be a final cause.

Let's look now at the second premise that seems false. There does not seem to be any reason why something which becomes more perfect, given enough time, will become a different kind of thing. It does not follow, for example, that if a species of bird develops a more perfect beak over many generations, then the beak will turn into a new and more perfect kind of organ altogether, like an eye or something else. There may be a range of possibilities outside of which no more development can take place within a species. Thus, we are not surprised when we find adaptation within a species for beak size and shape, but that is a different thing altogether from having no beak at all, or some other organ in place of a beak.

In fact, the opposite seems to be the case. The more perfect something becomes, the more firmly does it seem to be rooted in its kind, in its nature. Take a basketball player. Let's say he becomes as perfect as a basketball player can be, better than Michael Jordan. Does it seem likely that this process will result in him becoming a baseball player? No. The skills which perfect one for basketball often are opposed to the skills for other sports. Or take a man who becomes as perfect a man as he can be, both spiritually and physically. Is he now more easily able to be transformed into a woman, or into some other species of animal? Of course not. He is even less likely to become feminine or bestial. Again, take a car. When it has become perfect, having everything that a car should have and nothing that a car should not have, is it now more able to become an airplane or some other vehicle? No. Its perfections as a car make it more difficult to change it into another kind of vehicle.

On the other hand, when we see things in a state of imperfection, it is just then that they are more likely to change kinds. The seed of an orange tree is more like the seed of a lemon tree than the mature orange tree is like the mature lemon tree. An embryo of one species looks very similar to the embryo of another species. So it seems that when things are less perfect, they are more capable of being changed into one another. This is the opposite of the premise used in the argument for materialist evolution.

Last of all, notice that the premise that things can change from one kind of living thing into another presupposes that in fact there are substantially different kinds of living beings. But what kind of cause would be necessary to account for a change in kind or species? If there were a way of showing that living things could change from one kind to another, what kind of cause would have to be used in the argument? Well, the cause which makes a thing to be what it is, or the kind of thing it is: formal cause.

To be clear, there are certainly those who would object and say that one living thing really isn't more perfect than another, or different in kind than another. They would go so far as to say that human beings and amoebas are fundamentally the same kind of thing and one is just as good as another. But this is simply to deny that there is a problem which needs explaining. The whole reason why the theory of evolution was proposed in the first place was to explain different and better kinds of living things in terms of non-intelligent or purposeful causes. But to take refuge in the claim that things never were different or better after all does not explain the world we actually live in, but only explains it away. It is much like the arguments of Parmenides claiming that motion really didn't exist: those arguments ended up explaining away experience rather than explaining it.

After evaluating the argument for materialist evolution, we have found that two premises are not supported. Moreover, we have found that in order to reach the conclusion that there is evolution, material and agent causes are not enough. Formal and final causes would also be necessary. But if formal, and especially final causes are used to demonstrate that evolution takes place, this would not show that nature does not act for an end. Rather, it would show the opposite: that evolution itself is part of the way nature acts for an end!

Could Chance Be the Cause of the Appearance of Acting for an End in Nature?[27]

One objection we have not explicitly taken up is the position that chance causes the appearance of nature acting for an end. We all have the experience of seeing chance things taking place which seem to be done by design: a chance pattern in a rock formation looks like it was carved on purpose, a chance basket is made in a game when someone just deflected a pass into the basket, etc. Could chance explain nature acting for an end?

To answer this question, we need to define chance. Chance, as understood here, is a kind of cause. But what kind of cause? The kind of cause that makes things happen (like balls going through baskets) and forms things (like patterns in rocks). But the kind of cause that makes and shapes things is agent cause. So chance is a kind of agent cause. But not every agent cause is a chance cause. If someone intentionally made a basket, or intentionally carved a pattern in rock, this would not be done by chance. Chance things have to happen unintentionally (if they happened intentionally,

---

[27] Supplementary text: R. McInerny, *A First Glance at St. Thomas Aquinas*, ch. 9.

then chance causes would happen for an end, so chance causes would not be an alternative to nature acting for an end!). But it is not enough for a cause to act unintentionally if it is going to act by chance. Let's take a simple example: a man goes out for a walk every day, and every day (or nearly every day), he runs into the same person on his walk, even though he does not intend to do so. If this happened often enough, we would not credit their regular meetings to chance. Rather, we would look for an intentional cause: for example, the person might be a stalker. Similarly, if someone were to flip a coin and every time the coin came up heads, you would look for a true cause of this: for example, the coin might have two heads, or be weighted. Or if you were playing blackjack, and the dealer came up with a 21 every time, you would eventually suspect that he was cheating (however, if you think this is something that can always be explained by mere chance, I would like to play cards with you some time . . . bring lots of money). In other words, chance events not only happen unintentionally, they also happen rarely. Both are required for a chance cause.[28] So chance can be defined as *an agent cause which acts outside the intention of the agent and rarely.*

From this definition of chance, we can see why chance cannot be attributed to natural things as their true cause. Natural things happen always or for the most part, not rarely. When something happens always or for the most part, this is against the very definition of a chance event.

So if some seemingly chance event (e.g., some genetic mutation) seems to cause a new species or a new natural substance, this

---

[28] Notice too, that just because an event happens rarely, this is not sufficient to show that it is by chance. Treasure hunters rarely find treasure, but because they are intentionally looking for treasure, we do not attribute their finding treasure to chance.

does not explain the stability of the new species or substance, for unless the matter already has a natural aptitude to remain in a form, no mutation will explain why it stays and propagates in that new form. When things happen regularly, there is always something which is inclined to act regularly, and that inclination is an inclination for some determinate end, not chance.

What about the Original Problems with Nature Acting for an End?

While we have shown the materialist theory of evolution to be an insufficient argument, we have yet to respond to the principal objection raised to the position that nature acts for an end. Recall that asserting that nature acts for an end seems to be anthropomorphizing: human beings have purposes because they are intelligent. Doesn't it therefore follow that, if nature acts for an end, nature itself is intelligent?

The short answer to this question is: nature need not be intelligent to act for an end, so long as it is designed by something intelligent.[29] Artifacts like computers and cars have purposes and act for determinate ends, not because they are themselves intelligent, but rather because they were designed by man, who is intelligent. The same could be true about natural things as well. Nature and natural things act for an end in a different way than intelligent things do. Here's an illuminating text from Saint Thomas:

> Something by its own action or motion tends toward an end in two ways: in one way, as moving itself toward the end in the way a man does; in the other way, as moved by another toward the end, just as an arrow tends toward a determinate end from the fact that it is moved by the

[29] *Summa Theologiae*, I-IIae, q.1, a.2.

> archer, who by his action directs the arrow toward the end. Therefore, those things which have reason move themselves toward the end, since they have dominion over their acts through free will, which is a power of will and reason. But those things which lack reason tend toward an end through natural inclination as if moved by another, but not by themselves, since they do not know the notion of an end, and therefore are able to ordain nothing to an end, but are merely ordained toward an end by another. For the entire irrational nature is compared to God as an instrument to its principal agent.[30]

When we say that nature acts for an end, we do not mean to say that nature acts for an end the same way that a man does, or that there is final causality in nature in exactly the same way as there is final causality in human choices. Nevertheless, there are purposes for natural things which are the ultimate explanations for their being and coming to be.[31]

Some Other Problems with the Theory of Evolution

Besides these more universal problems with the argument for materialist evolution, there are more particular problems with the evidence that is usually brought forward to support not only materialist evolution, but any kind of evolution. For example, Darwin himself said that we should eventually be able to determine from an examination of fossils that all the species of animals developed gradually and imperceptibly, with no clear lines drawn between the various species of animals. In his own time, Darwin recognized that the fossil record was not like that, but still reflected distinct species of animals, without gradual

---

[30] *Summa Theologiae*, I-IIae, q.1, a.2, c.

[31] St. Thomas, *Commentary on the Physics*, Bk.II, lect. 12-14.

transitions between them. He attributed this to the insufficient number of fossils which had been gathered up until his time, and he expected those gaps to be filled as more fossils were discovered. However, even after millions upon millions of fossils have been gathered, we still observe the same gaps that existed in the fossil record in the time of Darwin.

A second, even more powerful objection to the theory of evolution is the position that some organs of living things are unable in principle to be developed gradually, but would have to be developed all at once. Recall that in order for some new organ to develop gradually over many generations, the small changes and adaptations inherited by the succeeding generations would have to give some advantage for survival. But if an organ is very complex, and none of its parts taken singly, or even most of them together, give any advantage for survival, there is no reason why these adaptations should be passed on to future generations. And so, some organs could not be developed as the result of random mutations through natural selection.

One good example of an organ of this kind is a light-sensitive organ like an eye. In order for such an organ to work, *all* of its various parts would have to be present together *at the same time in exactly the right arrangement*. Without everything being together at once, it simply won't work at all, and hence it will give no advantage for survival. Organs and organisms that are not able to be formed gradually, step-by-step, are said to have "irreducible complexity," since their complexity cannot be reduced back to simpler causes.

Finally, objectors point out that the processes of natural selection only work assuming you have living things which reproduce. Natural selection cannot be invoked to explain the origin of life itself or of living things. The reason is simple: natural selection assumes changes from one generation to the next, but if there are no generations, there are no changes from one generation to the next either. So there can be no selection of the fittest from each generation either.

Creation versus Evolution?

These difficulties with the theory of evolution, as it has been proposed by ancients (Empedocles) and moderns (Darwin) alike, seem to lead us to the conclusion that evolution is indeed impossible. Are we then led necessarily to the conclusion that God immediately created all the species of living things?

Well, that is a possibility, but we should be careful before asserting such things as certain or proven. Besides, it does not seem to be in keeping with the order of divine providence for God to create all the species of living things immediately without any intermediate or created causes. God typically wills in His providence to bestow the dignity of being causes upon creatures as well (since it makes His creatures more like Him, who causes all things). And theologians like Saint Augustine and Saint Thomas thought that creatures were involved as causes in the origins and the development of the various forms of life. Granted, these are theological reasons, based as they are on revelation, but truth harmonizes with truth. So perhaps there is a way that natural things themselves can contribute to their own development and perfection.

The first thing to see is that most of the arguments against evolution given above are not against evolution as such, but against *materialist* evolution: that is, an account of the development of the species of living things which does not allow for final causes (nor, consequently, for agents that act for ends, or for substantial forms). If some account could be given which does employ the other kinds of causes, this would overcome most of the objections given above.

A second thing to see is that, by asserting some form of evolution, we are not denying that God created the heavens and the earth at the beginning of time.[32] It is one thing to say that God created all the species of living things immediately and another thing to say that He created the heavens and the earth. For example, it is possible that God created the heavens and the earth, and in that act endowed the things He created with the power and inclinations to develop into the various species of living things. In this case, God would have created some things immediately, and other things would have come into existence through the mediation of created causes.[33]

Is Some Kind of Intelligence-Guided Evolution Possible?

There do remain three objections, however, which were raised against the possibility of evolution as such: the first was the gaps in the fossil records; the second was how to explain the origin of life itself; the third was how to explain those organisms which do not seem to be able to be developed gradually, step by step (organs or organisms that have "irreducible complexity").

---

[32] The Catholic Faith teaches that God created the universe in time (cf. *Catechism of the Catholic Church*, nos. 290–93). That is, the existing universe had a definite beginning in time. While this manner of creating is not able to be proved or disproved philosophically, nevertheless, it can be demonstrated using reason alone that God exists and that He is the Creator of all things. Creation in this sense means a relation of dependence of being of creatures upon the Creator. This kind of dependence could exist even if the universe existed from all eternity. So as far as the philosopher can judge, there are two possible ways in which the universe might have been created: from eternity, or in time. The Catholic Faith holds that only God has revealed that it was the latter and not the former.

[33] The Book of Genesis seems to speak this way when it says, for example, that God said, "Let the earth bring forth the living creatures in their kinds," etc. (Gn 1:24). This implies that God did not directly create these species, but brought them into being through the mediation of "the earth."

These difficulties are insurmountable if we hold to a natural universe without purpose and intelligent design. However, if the material elements of the universe are of such a nature that they have natural inclinations to self-organize, and act to dispose themselves to be formed as living things in the complex forms in which they now exist, it seems possible that some form of evolution could be responsible for the diversity of living things today. For example, if amino acids had natural inclinations to form into proteins, and other molecules had natural inclinations to form into DNA, then perhaps the origin of life could be explained in part by these natural inclinations and processes. Moreover, even the irreducibly complex organisms could be explained if there are specific inclinations which belong to the more basic forms of life to spontaneously organize into these complex systems. On such an account, the transformation would take place in a single generation and so would not likely be recorded in the fossil records.

But if matter is self-organizing, doesn't that mean that matter is the ultimate explanation after all, that nature does not necessarily act for an end, and that no intelligence needs to be posited as responsible for the order we find in living things? Quite the opposite: such an explanation would necessitate intelligence behind nature even more than an account in which every species is directly created. For the fact that the matter is perfectly disposed to act in this way is a further indication that the matter itself was the result of some intelligent design.[34] Let me give a simple example that will help to illustrate what I mean.

Let's say that your father comes home for Christmas with two toys. The first toy is a little robot which comes with a bag

[34] Supplementary text: St. Thomas, *Commentary on the Physics*, Bk. II, lect. 15.

of loose parts. Your dad dumps out the parts on the ground, turns on the robot, and the robot starts assembling the parts into other little robots, which in turn do the same thing. That is clearly a toy designed by an intelligent toymaker. The second toy is just a bag of parts. But when your dad dumps them out onto the ground, they start to assemble themselves into robots! Those robots then start assembling other robots from the remaining parts. Which toy would you think was designed by a more intelligent toymaker? Obviously the second, since he not only was able to make a robot that could assemble other robots, but he was even able to figure out how to design the parts so that they assembled themselves. Hence, if we were to one day discover that matter is self-organizing into these complex life forms, this would be evidence of an even greater intelligence behind the natural world.

All this is a big *if.* So far, no one has discovered any natural processes by which even a simple living organism might be produced on its own. Perhaps evolution is false, or perhaps some kind of evolution will one day be verified. But the important thing to realize is that the evolution vs. creation dichotomy is a red-herring (a false distraction that makes no difference to the conclusion you reach): either way, it is necessary to say that nature acts for an end, and that there is an intelligence behind the natural world.

Summary

- A theory of evolution which rejects final causality is contrary to reason. Some kind of final causality must be invoked to account for reality as it is.
- There are many strong objections to the modern theory of evolution as it is presented today.

- Nevertheless, it seems that some kind of evolution is possible, provided final causality in nature is admitted. Yet there are still serious difficulties that would have to be answered for any theory of evolution.
- The Christian doctrine of creation is not necessarily opposed to some forms of evolution.
- The existence of an intelligence behind nature is a necessary conclusion whether or not you hold for creation, evolution, or both.

CHAPTER 11

The Definition of Motion[35]

We have so far examined the definition of nature and the most universal principles and causes of natural things. It is time to return again to our definition of nature in order to understand that definition more fully and precisely. Among the terms in the definition of nature, the most important for our purposes is "motion." Therefore, the target of this chapter is to arrive at a definition of motion.

Is Motion Definable?

Motion is one of those words with which everyone feels very familiar. Motion is so much a part of our everyday experience that it would be hard to find an experience more common than that of motion. Like the air we breathe, it is all around us, and sometimes we don't even notice it because it is so commonplace. We are very certain of our experience of motion—as long as no one asks us what motion is, we know; yet if we want to explain it to someone who does ask us, we do not know what to say, we are at a loss for words. We would much rather point to the experience of motion than try to define it or account for it in words. If someone asks

[35] Supplementary texts: St. Thomas, *Commentary on the Physics*, Bk. III, lect. 1-2; and R. McInerny, *A First Glance at St. Thomas Aquinas*, ch. 11.

what motion is, it is easier to explain it by waving a hand in their face and saying: "Look! That's motion!"

This difficulty has led many thinkers to hold the position that the word "motion" is indefinable. For example, the father of modern philosophy, the seventeenth-century French philosopher René Descartes, says: "We call simple only those things the perception of which is so clear and distinct that they cannot be divided by the mind into many clear and distinct perceptions. Examples of these are: figure, extension, motion, and so on."[36] Likewise, the seventeenth-century English empiricist philosopher John Locke holds the same position, saying that one who inquires what motion is should go to his senses, since "the simple ideas we have are such as experience teaches them to us."[37]

However, it is abundantly clear that motion is in some way definable. First of all, we all know how to use the word "motion" correctly. And not everything is motion or a kind of motion, so motion is not coextensive with being. Motion must therefore be a certain kind of being: it must cut off, so to speak, a part of being. And if that is so, motion can at least be defined in terms of being and some difference added to being, specifying to what part of being motion belongs.

But those who have tried to define motion have often fallen into the trap of defining motion circularly: that is, defining it in terms of something else which itself is defined by motion. For example, to define motion as a "passing from one state of being to another," would be to define motion circularly, since "passing" is a certain kind of motion. If we were to define "passing" we would include motion in its definition.

---

[36] René Descartes, *Rules for the Direction of the Mind*, Rule 12.

[37] John Locke, *Essay Concerning Human Understanding,* ch. 4.

Getting a Genus of Our Definition of Motion

If we are going to define motion correctly, we are going to have to use all the tools we learned from logic and the art of defining. We will have to use, for example, the four marks of a good definition. And we will have to try to find the genus first, and the specific differences next.

A good place to start when looking for a genus is to go to the ten categories of being: substance, quantity, quality, etc. Perhaps one of these will be the genus of the definition of motion. Two good candidates seem to be acting upon and undergoing. But upon more careful reflection, neither seems to be the genus of motion. Some motions involve an acting upon, like heating, while other motions involve undergoing, like being heated. So neither genus seems universal enough to include all motion. In fact, when we look at the other categories, something similar happens. Locomotion is a change of place, so that belongs in the category of where. And alteration is a change of quality, so that belongs in the category of quality. And growth is a change in quantity, so that belongs in the category of quantity.

What we have discovered is that motion is such a universal phenomenon that it can't be neatly fit into one of the ten categories: it seems to belong in more than one, or possibly even in all the categories. What does this mean as far as the definition of motion is concerned? The first consequence of this is that motion must be a term which is used equivocally, not univocally. Remember that the categories are all univocal names. So if motion is in many categories, it will not be said univocally. A second consequence is that if our definition of motion is going to be coextensive with the term defined, the "genus" must be something more universal than one of the ten categories (I use the word "genus" in quotes because strictly speaking a genus is said univocally of the things under it, but here "genus" will be used in a looser sense, since the "genus" of motion will not be said univocally of the things under it).

So what could be our "genus" of motion? Let's look at another mark of a good definition: the defining terms must be better known than the term defined. So, our "genus" must be better known than motion. That seems like it's going to be tough to find. What could be better known than motion? But remember from logic: typically the term which is more universal is better known. What term is more universal than motion? Being. So let's begin there. Let's take being as our "genus." That's safe enough, since one thing we are sure about: motion is an existing thing.

Getting a Specific-Difference for Our Definition of Motion

Motion is a kind of being. To get down to motion from our "genus" of being, we need to divide the "genus" by a specific difference, or something that is like a specific difference. Of course, we have already seen that being is divided into the ten categories. But motion is not a being restricted to one of the ten categories, as we already saw above. Is there some other distinction or division of being that might be helpful in specifying what motion is? Besides this, such a distinction or division would have to be found in all the categories in which motion is found.

At this point it will be very helpful to go back to chapter four, where we asked whether motion was possible. The difficulties surrounding the existence of motion turn out to be the best starting point for refining our definition of motion. Recall that the key distinction which resolved the apparent contradiction about motion was the distinction of being into potential being and actual being. This distinction is universal, and is even found in each of the categories. For example, the category of substance can be divided into actual substance and potential substance (prime matter), and the category of quantity is divided into actual quantities (e.g., some line of a definite length) and potential quantities (e.g., the potential segments into which that line can be divided). So this distinction looks like the perfect starting place to look for a "specific difference" for our definition of motion.

So is motion the same as actual being? For example, is becoming red the same as actually being red? Or is becoming six feet tall the same as actually being six feet tall? No, those aren't the same. Something in motion is not yet actually that towards which it is moving. So motion is not the same as actual being. Well then, perhaps motion is the same as potential being. For example, is becoming red the same as being able to be red? Or is becoming six feet tall the same as being able to be six feet tall? That seems a little closer, but potential being still doesn't seem to be exactly the same thing as motion. For example, a green apple is able to be red, even when it is not in the process of ripening or moving towards red. Or someone who is not growing right now is still able to be six feet tall, so long as he grows sometime in the future. Or the player at rest on first base is able to be on second base, but so is the player running from first to second base. So potential being seems to be a bit broader than motion. To define motion as potential being would be too broad, since potential being includes motion and things not yet in motion.

Let's look at the example of the runner from first to second base again. When he's at rest on first base, he is able to be at second. When he's running from first to second base, he is also able to be at second base. But there is a big difference between those two abilities, those two potentialities. Which of the two abilities would you say is more real, more realized or actualized? The ability of the one who is in motion towards second base. He seems to be *more able* to be at second than the fellow who's just resting there at first. So motion seems to be a particularly actualized, or fulfilled, potency. The potency involved in motion is closer to being actual. Moving to red from green is closer to being actually red than just sitting there at green.

Let's take another example to help illustrate. If I hold a rock in my hand, that rock is able to be on the table. It is also able to be in any number of other places as well. It is actually in my hand, and potentially everywhere else. We could call this kind of potency to places other than my hand "pure" potency, since it is equally able to be anywhere else, and is not inclined or determined to be at one place rather than another. On the other hand, if I throw the rock towards the table, it is still able to be on the table, and theoretically, any other place, but it is more inclined to be on the table than on any other place. So long as it is moving towards the table, its potency to places other than the table is diminished: the rock is not equally able to be anywhere, since it has a special preference or inclination to go to the table rather than to some other place. Thus, when the rock is moving, its potency is no longer pure potency. It is an actualized or determined potency: one which is inclined more to one place than another. When the rock is at rest in my hand, it is able to be on the table, but when the rock is moving towards the table it is *really* able to be on the table. The potency to be on the table is most real just when it's moving there.

With this in mind, we can see that motion is a kind of potential being, but a special kind of potential being: an actualized potency. The way Aristotle expresses it is that motion is *the actualization of a thing in potency*, or more simply put, *the act of the potential.* Motion is not merely potency (that would be the rock in pure potency to another place), nor is it merely actuality (that would be the rock actually in the place it's resting), but it is something between these: that actuality of something in potency.

There is one last precision, just to clear up a possible misconception. If we say that motion is the act of the potential, someone might take this to mean it is the full realization of some potential that used to be there. For example, an apple is potentially red. Once it has become fully red, we can say that the potency to be red has been actualized. Thus, we can call the redness the act of the potential (i.e., the thing that *used to be* potential). Moreover, there is another possible way to misunderstand Aristotle's definition: while the apple is ripening to red from green, it is *actually* an apple throughout the entire motion. When Aristotle calls motion the act of the potential, he doesn't mean just any act (for example, the act of being an apple), he means that the potency itself is being actualized. To avoid these possible misinterpretations of his definition, Aristotle says that motion is *the act of the potential, insofar as it is potential.* That is, it is the act of something which is still in a state of potency, and an act precisely as related to its corresponding potency.

The "Species" of *Per Se* Motion

Now that we have arrived at a refined definition of motion, we are in a position to look back and see whether or not motion is in every category or only in some.

Aristotle concluded that there is no motion in the category of substance, strictly speaking. For motion demands that something be midway between potency and act. Yet there is no such midpoint in substantial change: substantial change is completed in an instant. There is never a time when something is between actual substances—it is either one substance or the other.

Aristotle also identified three categories in which motion is found *per se*, that is, in or through itself. Quantities, qualities, and places are things that can be changed in themselves. Other categories change because one of these others changes. For example, the relation of shorter changes to the relation of taller, because someone who used to be shorter than I am then grows and becomes taller than I am. That change in the category of relation happened through something else, namely through a change in the category of quantity.

So, in summary, motion in the category of quantity is called growth (if it is to something bigger) or shrinking (if it is to something smaller); motion in the category of quality is called alteration; and motion in the category of place is called locomotion. Of these three, locomotion has a certain priority, since the others somehow depend upon it.

A Test Case: Bertrand Russell's Definition of Motion

Now that we have a better understanding of the definition of motion, let's test your knowledge and see if you can identify what's wrong with the following definition of motion proposed by a philosopher named Bertrand Russell:

> Motion is simply being in one place at one time, being in another place at another time, and being at intermediate places at intermediate times.

(Hint: Use the four marks of a good definition to determine what's wrong with this definition.)

Summary

- Motion is definable, not a simple concept like being.
- While one verbal formula can be given for motion, motion is said equivocally by reason.
- The key distinction between act and potency is the distinction in terms of which motion is defined.
- There are three categories in which motion is found *per se*: quantity, quality, and place. Of these, locomotion (motion according to place) is primary.

CHAPTER 12

The Measures of Motion

Something can be made easier to understand if we see its causes or if we see its measures. For example, if we want to know something better, like an army, we can ask what it is for (final cause), or what it's made out of (material cause), or what arrangement of parts it has (formal cause), and so forth. To these questions we would get answers like: an army is assembled for winning a war, it is made of men over eighteen, and it has a general, footmen, and cavalry. These all answer questions about the causes of an army, and so they help us to understand an army better. But we can also understand something better when we understand its measures.

What is a measure? Well, the first sense of measuring something comes from using a ruler or something like a ruler to determine something else's length more accurately. We might have a vague idea of how wide a table is before we measure it, but if we want to find out if it will fit through a particular door, we might have to measure it and the door precisely. Or if I were in a room of people and I wanted to know exactly how many people were in the room, I would have to count them, and counting is another kind of measuring where we use a single thing as the unit (for instance a person would be the unit if we were counting persons, or an orange if we were counting oranges). And so, by measuring things, whether it be by counting or by placing a ruler up against it, or whatever, we come to know something better, or we come to know what we did not previously know.

With the case of our army, we would come to understand it better by measuring it. One way to measure an army is by counting the number of troops it has. This would be called an intrinsic measure, since it refers to the intrinsic size of the army itself. More often than not, this is one of the most important considerations about an army. An army of a thousand men and an army of ten thousand men makes quite a difference when planning strategy.

Another kind of measure is called an extrinsic measure. Extrinsic measures tell you more about the surroundings of a thing—for example, an extrinsic measure of an army might be the size of a place in which the army is situated. At the battle of Thermopylae, the Spartan army of only three hundred men was able to hold off the advancing Persian army of thousands because they were situated in a narrow pass. This extrinsic measure was an important factor in understanding how the Spartan army could fight against the Persian army.

Let's take some more examples. The volume of water in a container is the intrinsic measure of the water, whereas the amount of space inside the container is an extrinsic measure of that same water, since it is a measure not of the water, but of the container around the water (even if they happen to amount to the same quantitative value). The length of a table is its intrinsic measure, but the length of the yardstick placed along the table is an extrinsic measure: it tells you how long the table is from the outside. The same yardstick can be applied to a couch and a dresser.

Therefore, an intrinsic measure tells you about how much something is in itself—it belongs to the thing measured and only that thing. An extrinsic measure can be applied, like a ruler, to many different things in order to measure them.

In examining the definition of motion, we have considered the causes of motion in order to help us understand it better. For example, by looking at the term or endpoint of a motion (final cause), or by considering the mobile, that is, the thing which is in motion (material cause), or by considering the thing bringing the motion about (agent cause), we are able to understand a motion better. It remains for us to understand the measures of motion, if we wish to have a clear grasp of what motion is.

Motion has both intrinsic and extrinsic measures. For instance, the momentum or the kinetic energy of a body would be an intrinsic measure of its motion. Much of modern physics has concentrated upon these aspects of motion. On the other hand, there is another intrinsic measure of motion which is often overlooked in modern physics, but which Aristotle considered in depth. This measure is the infinite. Now no motion is actually infinite, but every motion is continuous. And because every continuous thing can be divided to infinity, every motion is in some way measured by the infinite, though not the *actually* infinite, but rather *the potentially* infinite. So one intrinsic measure of motion is the potentially infinite.

On the other hand, there are two chief extrinsic measures of motion. These are *time and place*. Time measures the before and after in motion, while place measures the limits of motion and the mobile. For instance, I can understand a trip better if I understand how long it takes (time), and the place that I'm leaving from and to which I am going. On an airline ticket, these are the facts which they give to the passenger so that he will understand the motion which will happen: departure city, departure time, arrival city, and arrival time. The idea of time and place as being measures of motion is already very familiar to us.

The following will be a brief treatment of the concepts of time and place which will help us to understand motion in general better.

Place

What is place? Like motion, it is a thing which I am very familiar with, yet if someone asks me to define it, I am at a loss for words. Everyone uses the word "place" without much difficulty: we say that the garage is the place of our car, and the church is the place of the altar, and so forth. It is easy to answer the question "what place is it in?" but it is not so easy to answer the question "what is place?"

Perhaps if we consider some of the characteristics of place, we will be in a better position to formulate a definition of place.

Now one characteristic of place is that it is always conceived together with a body. Only bodies are in a place. For example, we do not say that there is a place of truth or beauty or goodness or freedom or any of these things (or if we do, we are speaking metaphorically). Sometimes we say that a soul has a place, but only insofar as it is informing a body. In the same way, we might say that the color red has a place, but properly speaking, a red body, like an apple, is what has a place. And so we see that every place is the place of some body. We notice place most of all when we observe changes in place. For instance, when we drink a glass of water, the water has a new place (our stomach), while the old place, the glass, is filled with another body (namely air). So we see from this that place is something distinct from a body, since one and the same body can have different places and one and the same place can contain different bodies.

The reality of place is further confirmed by the fact that place seems to have a real power to attract things. For instance, heavy things tend to move towards lower places while light things tend to move towards higher places.

Many thinkers have seen that there are numerous difficulties in understanding the concept of place. A brief look at some of these difficulties will help us to understand the definition of place better.

First of all, if place is something, it seems that it must be a body. For place seems to be extended in three dimensions, since it has depth, width, and length. But only bodies have three dimensions; therefore, place seems to be a body. But if this is true, then it would follow that when a body is in a place, two bodies would exist together (that is, they would coincide), for the place in which the body is, is also a body. But it is impossible for two bodies to coincide.

Secondly, whatever exists must be a cause of something in some way. But place cannot be a cause in any of the four senses of cause. For place cannot be a material cause, since a material cause remains in that of which it is a cause, but place does not remain in things, since anything can be moved from one place to another. Place cannot be a formal cause, because formal cause makes a thing to be what it is, but different things can occupy the same place without becoming the same. Place cannot be an agent cause, because those places which seem to cause motions are at the endpoint of those motions rather than at the beginning. Last of all, place cannot be a final cause, since it seems that places exist for the sake of things which are in place rather than vice versa. Therefore, since place cannot be a cause in any of these ways, it seems that place does not exist.

Thirdly, it seems that every material thing is in a place. But place seems to be a material thing. Therefore, it follows that every place is itself in a place, and so on to infinity. But this is absurd. Therefore, it seems to follow that there is no such thing as place.

Fourthly, place seems to be some kind of space or void, which is extended in three dimensions without containing a sensible body. But quantity is always a quantity of some substance, for it answers the question "how much?" Therefore, it seems that there can be no such thing as place.

Fifthly, place seems to be something stable and immovable: for we do not say that a place changes place, but rather that something changes from one place to another while the places remain. But many things seem to have place even though their surroundings are always changing. For instance, a boat docked on a river seems to remain in place even though the water of the river moves around the boat.

These are some of the difficulties associated with place. Some thinkers first attempted to solve these difficulties by defining place as the matter or as the form of something. But both matter and form are intrinsic to a thing, while place is extrinsic to a thing. This is why when a thing moves, we say that its matter and form move with it, but its place does not. For nothing can go outside of its own matter or its own form, but something can go outside of its place. Therefore, it is impossible for place to be matter or form.

Aristotle mentions that we know that we have defined something most perfectly when we are able to resolve all of the difficulties around it by means of the definition. And this is true of the definition of place which Aristotle proposes. This definition of place is *the first, immobile surface of the containing body.*

It is clear that place is something of the *containing body* because whenever we say where something is, we always indicate the containing body. For instance, where is the student? He is in the classroom. Where is the water? It is in the glass.

And if we want to know exactly where something is, we find *the first surface* which contains it. For instance, I might want to know where my place is at the baseball game. It is not enough to say "Dodger Stadium" or "Level 1" or "Section 49" or "Row C." I would have to give the exact seat number as well in order to accurately specify my place. These other places are in fact places, but they are called common places, as opposed to a thing's proper place, which is what we are defining.

But what is the reason for the additional word *immobile* in the definition of place? The reason for this is that sometimes a body is surrounded by moving things, like a fish underwater or a boat in a river. While the water is moving, the fish or boat may actually be at rest with respect to the shore, and so the first containing surface of the fish or boat which is immobile would be the shore of the river. In that case, the proper place of the boat is the riverbed (that is, the shore), since this is the first surface which contains the boat and yet is not moving.

This understanding of how place is immobile brings up the distinction between motion *per se* (through itself) and motion *per accidens* (through what happens to a thing). When a man is walking, he is in motion *per se*, but his tooth is only in motion *per accidens*, since the tooth is simply being carried along as a part of the whole man. This distinction between motion *per se* and motion *per accidens* is different from relative and absolute motion. A thing is in motion absolutely when it is under the influence of some kind of agent, while something is in relative motion when, although not being acted upon by any agent, it is compared to something. Thus, when I move my index finger, my finger is in motion absolutely, while the rest of the universe is in relative motion to my index finger. As this example illustrates, relative motion is not really motion at all, but rather a comparison which the mind makes.

Discuss in class how the definition of place solves all the aforementioned difficulties.

Time

Time is another difficult notion to grasp. Time is an extrinsic measure of motion, similar to the way in which place is an extrinsic measure of body, but time is less stable than place. Place seems to be constant, but time is always changing.

Someone might ask: Can time exist without motion? At least at first glance this does not seem unreasonable. But if we consider our experience, we will find that motion and time are necessarily joined. For whenever we sense or experience motion, we perceive time. And even when we do not sense some particular motion, as when we are in the dark and it is quiet, still, as soon as we notice a succession of our thoughts or something like this, we perceive time at once. But when we sleep or do not perceive any motions at all, it seems as if no time has passed. Therefore, time, insofar as we experience it, is never experienced apart from motion.

For this reason, some have been led to believe that time is the same thing as motion. But this does not conform to our experience. For motions are in the things which are moved, while time seems to be everywhere and among all things. Also, motions are either fast or slow, but time seems to move evenly. For this reason, we determine whether a particular motion was fast or slow by comparing the motions to time, as if time were a common standard or measure by which any particular motion can be measured. For example, we say that a faster car is one which travels the same distance in a shorter time.

Since time is not motion, but time is always together with motion, it follows that time is some property of motion: that is, time is something which is always associated with motion, just as, for example, transparency is always associated with water or place is always associated with a body.

Moreover, there seems to be some kind of irreversible order in time. For time seems to flow continuously from the future into the past, without change of direction.

After taking into account all these characteristics of time, Aristotle defines time as *the number of motion according to before and after*. He says that time is something *of motion* since time is always together with motion and is always related to it.

Aristotle calls time a *number* because time seems to be a kind of measure of motion. For we judge something to be more or less by its number, but we judge motions to be more or less by their times, and therefore, time is *the number of motion*. And even though time is continuous just as the motions which time measures are continuous, still there is always a discrete element to the way in which time measures motion. When someone measures a piece of fabric with a yardstick by counting the number of yards of fabric, he is using numerical measures even though both the yardstick and the fabric are continuous.

Aristotle says that time is a measure *according to before and after* to indicate that there is an order in time. And this order is consequent upon the before and after found in motion. For example, we say that the daytime is after the sunrise and before the sunset, while nighttime is after the sunset and before the sunrise.

But it still remains to be seen why it is that time seems to be something which seems to be everywhere and which flows independently of the particular motions which we sense. The answer to this question is that there is one first motion which is the cause of all other motions. Things are said to be simultaneous which are moved together by the same cause, and since there is a first motion which is the cause of all motions, each one of these particular motions can be compared by referring it back to this first motion. In this way, the time which is the number of that first motion is the universal time by which all motions are measured. Aristotle thought that this first motion was the rotation of the sphere of the stars about the earth, but we now know that this is not true. And so it remains to be discovered what this first motion, or first mobile cause of motion, is.[38]

[38] Some possible explanations for the seeming ubiquity and uniformity of time include the natural and universal upper limit upon velocity (the speed of light), or perhaps even the psychological experience of a constant rotation of the earth as a basis for an internal, constant awareness of the equal flow of time. Some have even posited the constant rate of expansion of the universe as a possible cause for the experience of the equal flow of time (see, for example, "The Ground and Properties of Time" by R. Glen Coughlin, in *The Aquinas Review*, vol.19 [2013-14] p.23-78). However, because this is an introductory course, we leave these questions uninvestigated.

CHAPTER 13

The Divisibility of Motion and Mobile

Lines Are Not Composed of Points

The title of this section may seem strange, especially if you have read a modern math book and supposedly learned that a line *is* composed of points. But the authority of any math book has to give way to experience of the real world, and our experience teaches us that a line is not composed of points. Here's how we know that: a point has no size and no parts. Therefore, a point can't be exactly next to another point so that it touches the next point or overlaps the next point. If it overlapped the point next to it, then it would have to have a part which overlaps, but points have no parts. Again, if a point just touched the next point over, it would have to have a surface which touched, but that means a point would have parts (a surface distinct from the rest of the point). Thus, if a point touches a point, it completely coincides with it. They are exactly in the same position. And no matter how many points you put there (even an infinite number, if that were possible), you still get a point in that one position. On the other hand, if you put a point near to a point but not on it, then there will always be some distance between the two points, since they can't touch or overlap. So you can't make a line up from points: a line will always be between points, but it won't be composed from points. This fact will be helpful in the next section about the infinite and motion.

The Infinite as a Measure of Motion

We have already considered time and place, which are the extrinsic measures of motion. Here we will briefly consider the infinite which is a kind of intrinsic measure of motion. Recall that it is not the *actually* infinite but the *potentially* infinite which is a kind of intrinsic measure of motion, since every motion is continuous and therefore potentially divisible to infinity. How do we know this? Because every mobile is continuous and potentially divisible to infinity. But how do we know this?

We can make a *reductio ad absurdum* (reduction to the absurd) argument to prove that every mobile, and hence every motion, is continuous and divisible to infinity. The way a *reductio ad absurdum* argument works is by assuming that the opposite of the conclusion we want to prove is true. Then based upon that assumption, we demonstrate something which is clearly false. So let's assume the opposite of the statement "every mobile is continuous." That is, let's assume that something indivisible, like a point, can move. Will this result in some absurdity? Let's find out.

Wherever an indivisible thing is, it must be wholly there, not partly there and partly somewhere else. The reason is that an indivisible thing has no parts, so it can't have one part in a place and another part outside that place, or it can't be partly red and partly green. Wherever or whatever it is, it has to be wholly there: all or nothing. Now whatever is wholly where it is or wholly what it is, is fully actual regarding that place or attribute. For example, whatever is wholly in a particular place is actually in that place, not potentially there. And whatever is wholly red is actually red, not potentially red. But this means that motion is impossible for that indivisible thing, since whatever is in motion is between pure potency and pure act, since motion is the act of the potential insofar as it is potential.

The only possibility for an indivisible thing is to be at one point at one time, and suddenly at another point at another time (remember two points can't be right next to each other, there always has to be some distance between them). So for an indivisible thing to change locations, it would have to disappear from one place, and suddenly reappear at another. Two absurdities follow from this. First, the "motion" of this indivisible thing would be composed of rests, since at no point during the process would the thing be moving; it would always be resting where it is. Second, the indivisible thing would constantly be annihilated and recreated as it changed locations from point to point. Since neither of these absurdities can be reconciled with our experience, we must hold the opposite of what we at first assumed. Therefore, every mobile must be continuous. And every motion must also be continuous, since motion is something of the mobile.

As we shall see in later chapters, this conclusion will be important in demonstrating the conclusion that every thing which is in motion, is moved by something else.

Another interesting conclusion that follows from what we have stated is that there can be no first moment of a motion: there can only be a last moment of rest before the motion begins. In class, see if you can establish why this must be the case.

CHAPTER 14

Where Does Natural Philosophy Lead Us?

At the beginning of this year, we considered the question: "What is philosophy?" After some discussion, we came to a general consensus that philosophy is a kind of explanation or account of reality: *an account of reality in terms of its ultimate causes insofar as these causes are discoverable by reason*. What is true of the whole is also true of the part. For just as philosophy in general is concerned with explaining the ultimate causes of reality, so also natural philosophy is concerned with explaining the ultimate causes of natural things in particular. That is, natural philosophy aims at understanding the ultimate causes of motion and mobile beings.

And so, for the person who is seeking to understand the world of nature, it is necessary to determine if there is an ultimate cause of natural things. And if so, he must determine if there is one cause or many. Furthermore, he must attempt to discover the nature and properties of this ultimate cause, for the more perfectly he understands the first cause or causes of nature, the better will he understand nature itself.

Aristotle takes up this task in the last two books of his work *Physics*. The following is a brief summary of his main arguments and conclusions.

Is There a First Cause of Motion?

Aristotle shows that there is a first cause of motion by the following argument: Everything which is in motion, is in motion because it is being moved by something else. And so we observe in nature a series of movers and things being moved. Now either this is traced back to something which is first in causing other things to move, or there is an infinite series of movers and moved things. If we take the second option, then there is no first thing which moves the others. But if each thing is in motion because it is being moved by something before it, and if there is no first thing causing a motion, the intermediate things will also not cause motions, and so nothing will be in motion, which is clearly false. This is called the problem of infinite regress. To take an example, if I move a rock with a stick, and the stick is moved by my hand and my hand is moved by my arm, and I keep going backwards in this way without end, I will never come to anything which is responsible for moving my arm or my hand or the stick or the rock, and so none of them will be in motion. For however many intermediates there are, all of them can be considered as if they were one intermediate moved, mover. Therefore, from this it is clear that the only reasonable option is that there is some first thing which is responsible for the motion of other things. But this first thing cannot be in motion itself, otherwise it too would need something else to move it. Therefore, this first thing which is responsible for motion must be immobile, that is, immovable.

Is this first thing God? Not necessarily, at least not according to this argument. For it suffices that the series of movers and moved things terminate at something which is not itself in motion. Now the human soul (or an angel, if such things can be shown to exist) is like this.[39] For although the human soul can cause the limbs of its body to move, it does not do so insofar as it is in motion. Let us take an example from everyday experience. When I pick up a pen to write, the pen is moved by my hand, and my hand is moved by my arm, and the arm is moved by the contraction of certain muscles, and the muscles contract as a result of certain nerve impulses, and these nerve impulses come from the brain. But ultimately, what starts everything in motion is the choice which I make. As soon as we make the choice, everything else gets set into motion: the nerve impulses are sent, the muscles contract, the arm moves the hand, the hand grasps the pen, and the pen writes. And, provided that our choice was made freely, there does not seem to be anything before this choice which causes the motion of the pen. Our choice is, in a sense, the ultimate reason for the motion of the pen.

There are some important distinctions which we still need to make. Later on, for example, we shall see that it is necessary to say that there is an uncreated first principle of motion, namely God, Who is active even in our choices. But this is a long way from being demonstrated.

On the other hand, a more immediate objection can be raised. We said before that the first cause of motion must itself be immobile, but a human soul seems to be moveable, since our soul is where our body is, and our body moves from place to place. To solve this problem, it is necessary to distinguish between motion *per se,* and accidental motion. A thing is moved *per se* when it is moving in and of itself. A thing is moved accidentally when it is moved only because it happens to be with something which

39 At this point, we are not assuming that the soul is immaterial, or immortal, but rather we are simply calling the principle of motion in a man his soul, whatever that principle may be, material or immaterial.

is moved *per se*. Now the only reason we say the soul is moved is because the body is moved. The body changes place, or grows, or is moved in some way *per se*. But the soul changes place or grows or moves only accidentally, since it happens to be the soul of the body which undergoes these changes. The soul doesn't have a place of itself, nor does it grow when the body grows. Therefore, properly speaking, only the body is moved in these ways. And so while the soul is moveable in an accidental way, it is *per se* immobile. Therefore, the soul qualifies as an immobile mover: namely, something which causes other things to move without itself being in motion *per se*.

So in summary, there must be some mover or movers which put other things into motion, but are not themselves in motion, and such a thing might be a human soul or an angel or God or something else like these.

The Proof That Everything Which Is in Motion Is Moved by Something Else

Let us return to Aristotle's main argument. For everything we have said so far depends upon the truth of the first premise which Aristotle laid down: everything which is in motion is in motion because it is moved by something else. In the above example, this is clear: as I pick up a pen, the pen is in motion because my hand is moving it, and my hand is in motion because my arm is moving my hand, and so forth. In such cases it is obvious that the things which are in motion are being moved by something other than themselves.

But there are some cases which seem to pose difficulties with this statement. For some things manifestly move themselves: most notably animals, but also falling bodies and projectiles. These seem to be moving without anything causing their motions. In such cases it is hard to say whether or not there is some cause of their motion other than themselves. The statement that everything which is in motion is moved by something else is therefore not self-evident but needs to be proved.

The proof for this position is as follows:

> Every mobile is continuous, that is, it can be divided, at least conceptually, into any number of parts.
>
> But whatever has parts is either moved because its parts are moved or it is moved by itself as a whole.
>
> If the mobile were not in motion because of its parts, then it would follow that stopping a part would not stop the whole.
>
> But experience tells us that if a part of a mobile is stopped, the whole will be stopped. For example, if I am walking and someone holds my arm at rest, my whole body will be brought to a stop.
>
> Therefore, every mobile is moved in virtue of its parts, and not by itself as a whole.
>
> And since every part of a mobile is itself divisible, (for the definition of the continuous is that which is infinitely divisible into parts), it follows that no part of any mobile will be in motion in virtue of itself as a whole. Therefore, no mobile will be in motion through itself, but it will have to be moved by something else.
>
> And since there is nothing within the mobile which explains its motion, this means that the source of motion must be something outside of the mobile.

The proof that every mobile is continuous is as follows:

> If something did not have parts, it would not be subject to motion.
>
> This is shown as follows: every motion is from one thing to another thing.
>
> But when a mobile is in the terminus of a change, it has already finished being changed; therefore, it is not moving.
>
> For nothing is being changed and already changed at the same time.
>
> And for the same reason, when a mobile is in the beginning point of a motion, it has not yet begun to move.
>
> Therefore, something is not moving if the whole of it is at the beginning point or the end point of a motion.
>
> Thus, as any motion is starting, part of the mobile must be in the beginning point, and part of it outside the beginning point: for example, when a stone is first being moved, part of it is outside the place which it originally occupied, while the remainder is inside of the place which it originally occupied.
>
> But if something has no parts, it cannot have one part outside the beginning point and another within the beginning point of the motion.
>
> Rather, a mobile which has no parts must be wholly within the beginning point or the terminus (that is the proximate terminus, not necessarily the ultimate terminus—as in the change from white to black the proximate terminus is grey).

> And therefore, something having no parts must simply cease being one thing and start being another, for example, it must cease being white and start being grey, and this is not a motion.
>
> For it goes immediately from being actually white to actually grey, without any in-between.
>
> But motion is the act of something potential, therefore, since something which has no parts would go immediately from being one thing in act to being another thing in act, it follows that it was never in motion.

Syllogistic breakdowns of the arguments that nothing in motion is moved by itself and that every mobile is moved by something else are provided at the end of this chapter.

Response to Some Difficulties

The above arguments show that everything which is in motion is moved by something else. It now remains to respond to the difficulties with the self-movement of animals, heavy bodies, and projectiles.

In animals, the solution to this difficulty is like the case of a man who moves himself. For an animal has parts, namely its sense organs, which move its other parts, such as the muscles and limbs. The sense organs of an animal are in turn moved by something outside of the animal. For example, the smell of food causes a series of reactions in the body of the animal which result in the movement of the animal towards the food. Whether or not an animal has a soul which can be the first principle of an animal's motion as a human soul can be would have to be demonstrated. But at this point, it suffices to show that an animal is moved by something other than itself: either something outside of it, or by something like a soul which is itself immobile.

With regard to heavy bodies or projectiles, it is clear that such things are not the cause of their own motion, since they are not able to cause their own rest. For if something causes an effect, when the cause is removed, the effect is removed. Therefore, if a body were able to move itself, it would also be able to bring itself to rest. But in heavy bodies and in projectiles, it is evident that these never bring themselves to rest. Rather something outside them brings them to rest. Besides this, it is obvious from experience that heavy bodies and projectiles are always put into motion by some external cause. And so we must conclude that it is not in the power of such things to move themselves. The question remains: what is the thing outside of them which causes their motion? In the case of a projectile, it is obvious that the beginning of the motion is always due to some external agent, yet it is not clear whether any agent is responsible for the continuance of their motion. In the case of heavy bodies, it seems that there is an attraction between bodies like that observed with a magnet and iron, but it is not obvious how this comes about or whether one thing can act upon another to cause it to move from a distance.

The identification of particular agent causes in these cases is difficult, and various theories have been proposed to account for the continued motion of projectiles and other bodies. However, the demonstrations set forth by Aristotle from common and certain experience manifest that there must be *some* cause outside of the mobile which is responsible for its continued motion (see the argument that every mobile is moved by another at the end of this chapter). To deny this solely because such a cause is not manifest or sensible, or because such a cause is not well understood, is not a good argument. By the same kind of argument, the existence of atoms and molecules, or germs and viruses, could have been denied two hundred years ago. In view of the principle that the mover and moved must be in contact, it seems that the medium through which a mobile travels must be responsible for some kind of agency upon the mobile. Great physicists such as Einstein held this position.[40] But since this question pertains to a more detailed investigation of particular natural causes, it is not appropriate to consider these causes in an introductory text. Suffice it to say, it is clear that mobiles such as heavy bodies and projectiles can be explained in terms of external agents, and this overcomes the objection that they must be self-movers.

What Is This First Cause Like, and Is There Just One, or Are There Many?

After having shown that there must be some first mover or movers which is/are immobile, Aristotle proceeds to determine more accurately what the nature of this first mover is like, and whether it can be determined if there is one or many such unmoved movers. This is the purpose of the eighth and last book of the *Physics*. The following is a summary of Aristotle's argument, together with my own comments and observations.

The first observation Aristotle makes is that if motion exists now, it must have always existed. Here is how he reasons: Let us suppose that at some time nothing was in motion. Then if everything was peacefully at rest, there would be no way to put anything into motion. For nothing which is at rest moves unless something puts it into motion. Therefore, since it is obvious that

---

[40] Einstein posited an immobile medium which was somehow responsible for the motion of things passing through it. For example, see his article entitled "The Inadequacy of Classical Models of Aether." He even concludes the article by asserting that "[i]n accordance with the general theory of relativity space without an ether is inconceivable."

there is motion, it must be true that things have always been in motion.

This kind of reasoning may at first seem fallacious to someone who accepts Christian revelation. After all, Christian revelation teaches that the world was created at some past point in time, so that motion must not have always existed. But let us consider what Aristotle was attempting to discover. He was trying to discover *solely from what could be known by reason* what the first cause of motion and mobile things is. It is true that he could have assumed that the world was created by God at some previous time, but this would have been an unphilosophical way of reasoning: it would have assumed what he was trying to prove. So he prefers to take the only route which is accessible by reason in this proof.

With these things having been said, we can reformulate the argument as follows:

> Either the world is eternal, or it began in time.
>
> If it began in time, there must be a universal cause of all matter coming to be from nothing, so that there must be a Creator of the universe who makes all things to have being in their proper order.
>
> On this assumption, we have already arrived at a first, universal cause of all motion and mobile beings who is eternal, free, and intelligent, and this is what we call God.
>
> But on the other hand, if the world is eternal then either:
>
> 1. it was at some time at rest and then put into motion by something outside of it, or
>
> 2. it has always been in motion.

> If we take option one, there must be some first cause of all motion who decided at some time to put the world in motion.
>
> And therefore, we are led back to the thesis that there is a God who is eternal and who directs all things.
>
> On the other hand, if we accept option two, it still remains to be seen whether or not some first eternal, free, and intelligent being is necessary to explain the universe.

And this last option is the one which Aristotle investigates since the others are not provable by reason.

Therefore, taking the position that the universe has always existed and that it has always been in motion, Aristotle continues with his argument. If motion has eternally existed, and, as we have already shown, there must be some first unmoved cause or causes of this motion, then either:

1. there is one ultimate and necessary unmoved mover which has existed eternally, or
2. there is a series of contingent unmoved movers (that is non-eternal and non-necessary causes) which are responsible for the motion of the universe.

If we take the second option, then there must be an infinite series of non-necessary beings which successively come to be and pass away (like men or animals), which take turns at causing motion in the universe. But this cannot be true. For every necessary effect must depend upon a necessary cause, just as a necessary conclusion in an argument must depend upon necessary premises. Multiplying contingent premises will not get a necessary conclusion, nor will multiplying contingent movers get a necessary motion. The person who says that an infinite series of contingent movers explains eternal generation and motion is caught in a circular argument: why is there eternal generation and motion? Because there are an infinite series of movers which are eternally generated in succession. And why are there an infinite series of movers which are eternally generated in succession? Because there is eternal generation and motion. Such an argument is clearly fallacious. Therefore, if motion is eternal (and hence, necessary), there must be some eternal and necessary cause of motion, and there need only be one of these since to posit more than one would be superfluous.

Now since there is an eternal being which causes the motion of the universe, and since this motion has existed forever, it follows that this mover must have an infinite power. For a finite power is required to move something for a finite time, but an infinite power is required to move something for an infinite time. From this Aristotle reasons that this first, eternal, unmoved mover must not have a body: for an infinite power cannot exist in a body, since every body is finite.

And so we have come to the conclusion that there must be some first, universal cause of all motion, and that this cause is eternal and necessary, and that it is separated from a body, that is, it is immaterial. At this point, Aristotle ceases his investigation. The reason for this is that natural philosophy is about natural things (things which are material or at least in matter). And since he has proven that this first mover is not in motion or material in any way, it does not fall to natural philosophy to investigate its essence or properties.

But since this introduction to philosophy does not include a section on first philosophy (or metaphysics, as it is more commonly called), let us at least briefly summarize what the attributes of such a being would be. Such an immaterial first cause seems to be a mind of some kind, since it moves and puts order into all things, and it must do this from the order which it possesses in itself (i.e., by way of knowledge). Therefore, this first being must be all-knowing and all-powerful. And this first cause must also be all-good. For it is the origin and source of all motion as the agent cause, and since every agent acts for an end, it must act for some good. But this good cannot be something outside of itself, otherwise there would be something which it was lacking. But the origin of all being cannot lack anything. Therefore, the first agent cause is also the ultimate final cause—that is to say, it is the ultimate good of the universe. This first being is what men call God.

Syllogistic Breakdown of the Argument That Nothing in Motion Is Moved by Itself[41]

2) Everything being moved by itself is mover and moved at once	All A is B
3) Nothing in motion is mover and moved at once	No C is B
1) Nothing in motion is moved by itself	No C is A

4) Everything which is mover and moved at once is in act and ability in the same respect at the same time	All A is B
5) Nothing is in act and ability in the same respect at the same time	No C is B
3) Nothing in motion is mover and moved at once	No C is A

6) ***Everything being moved is led from ability to act***	All A is B
7) Everything being led from ability to act is still in ability	All B is C
4a) Everything being moved is in ability	All A is C

8) Every mover gives act to something in ability	***All A is B***
9) Everything which gives act to something in ability is in act	***All B is C***
4b) Every mover is in act	All A is C

[41] Self-evident and necessary statements are printed in italics and boldface.

Syllogistic Breakdown of the Argument That Every Mobile Is Moved by Another[42]

1) Every mobile is continuous	All A is B
2) Whatever is continuous is moved by something other than itself	All B is C
3) Every mobile is moved by something other than itself	All A is C
4) Whatever is continuous is divisible into parts	All A is B
5) Whatever has parts is moved in virtue of those parts, not through itself	All B is C
2) Whatever is continuous is moved by something other than itself	All A is C
6) If something having parts were not in motion in virtue of its parts, then stopping a part would not stop the whole	If A then not B
7) But stopping the part does stop the whole	B is so
5) Whatever has parts is moved in virtue of those parts	Not A
8) Whatever is not continuous cannot move	All C is not B
9) Every mobile can move	All A is B
1) Every mobile is continuous	All A is not C
10) Whatever is wholly in the beginning or terminus of a motion cannot move	All B is not C
11) Something which is indivisible is wholly in that in which it is	All A is B
12) Something which is indivisible is cannot move	All A is not C
13) Whatever is not continuous is indivisible	All A is B
12) Something which is indivisible cannot move	All B is C
8) Whatever is not continuous cannot move	All A is C

[42] Self-evident and necessary statements are printed in italics and boldface.

14) Whatever is wholly in the beginning or terminus of a motion is fully in act with respect to that beginning or terminus All A is B

15) Whatever is fully in act cannot be in motion with respect to that act All B is not C

10) Whatever is wholly in the beginning or terminus of a motion cannot move with respect to that beginning or terminus All A is not C

16) Motion is the act of a potential thing insofar as it is potential All C is B

17) Whatever is fully in act cannot be the act of a potential thing insofar as it is potential All A is not B

15) Whatever is fully in act cannot be in motion with respect to that act All A is not C

CHAPTER 15

Demonstrations for the Existence of God[43]

Besides the argument given above in the previous chapter, there are other arguments which come to substantially the same conclusion. This is a brief explanation of some of these other arguments for God's existence. Before explaining these arguments, it is important to know some things in advance about the various kinds of knowledge. Not all knowledge is the conclusion to an argument. If that were the case, then the premises upon which each conclusion depends would themselves have to be proved by another argument using other premises, and these other premises would have to be proved in turn, and so on to infinity. So to know anything would require that an infinite number of premises be known. And since the human mind cannot know an infinite number of statements, it follows that nothing would be known, if all knowledge were the conclusion to an argument. Therefore, it remains that some truths can be known in themselves, without an argument. These truths are called "self-evident," since they do not depend upon something outside of them to be known.

---

[43] Supplementary texts: Michael Augros, *Aquinas on Theology and God's Existence: The First Two Questions of the Summa Theologiae Newly Translated and Carefully Explained*. Editiones Scholasticae: 2019.

A proof is certain and conclusive when the form of the argument is valid and the premises upon which the conclusion rests are self-evident and necessary. So if a proof for God's existence is shown to be conclusive, it must be based upon self-evident and necessary premises which are in the form of a valid syllogism. Therefore, the first thing we have to determine is how to tell when a statement is self-evident or not.

To say that a statement is self-evident is not the same thing as saying that it is self-evident *to everyone*. Let's take some examples. A man gets in his car to drive somewhere. It is self-evident to him that he is intending to drive to the store, but it is not evident to anyone else. His wife, for example, would have to take his word for it. Again, it is self-evident to a man from a cold climate that ice floats on water, or that water turns into ice. But for the person who has no experience of these things, it is not evident. To the man who fasts habitually, it is self-evident that fasting reduces concupiscence, but not to the man who has no experience of fasting. So the first thing to realize is that a statement may be self-evident to one person, but not to another, since the other person may be lacking experience of the things signified by the statement or he may be lacking an understanding of the meaning of the words in that statement.

The proofs we aim to consider for God's existence are proofs which depend upon statements about common experience (experiences had by all men so long as they are aware of their surroundings). For example, the experience of motion, the experience of cause and effect, the experience of order, the experience of goodness, are all common experiences. Everyone has these experiences. Therefore, what is necessary for the student to come to see the premises of these proofs as self-evident, is an understanding of the meaning of the words (for example, the definition of motion, or the definition of order, etc.).

The premises in a strict proof must also be necessary, since nothing gives what it doesn't have, and non-necessary premises cannot give someone necessary knowledge of a conclusion. In our logic course, we have already seen that in necessary statements the predicate must belong to the subject on account of the subject itself (*per se*), and that there are three kinds of *per se* statements. The first kind of *per se* statement is one in which the predicate is in the definition of the subject (e.g., a bachelor is unmarried). The second kind of *per se* statement is one in which the subject is in the definition of the predicate (e.g., every number is even or odd). The third kind of *per se* statement is one in which the predicate follows from the subject as from its immediate cause (e.g., the swimming man got wet). In the following proofs for God's existence, see if you can identify the self-evident premises and determine which kind of *per se* statement each one is.

Another thing which must be kept in mind is that, if we are going to prove anything to be true about God, we must have a definition of God. Recall too that there are three kinds of definitions: essential definitions (from the causes of a thing), definitions by property (from the effects of a thing), and nominal definitions (telling merely what the name means). It is clear that we cannot have an essential definition of God, since that would require that God be caused by something. But if God is supposed to be the absolutely first cause, it is clear that God has no cause. Therefore, our definition of God must be a definition from effects or a nominal definition. But we can't *start* with a definition from effects, since we don't know at the beginning of the argument whether or not God actually exists. And something that doesn't exist doesn't have any effects. So we have to use as our starting point a nominal definition of God: a definition which signifies what the name "God" means. It may not be that everyone will agree to every nominal definition: this is one reason why it is useful to have several nominal definitions. But all of the nominal definitions at least need to be a reasonable account of what the name "God" means in common speech.

One last remark before we proceed to the proofs themselves: these proofs aim to prove that God *exists*, not all of God's other attributes (for example, that God is all-wise, or all-powerful, or the father of Jesus Christ, etc.). For that matter, these proofs don't even show that there is only one God as opposed to many gods. Those things may be true, but they would have to be the conclusions of other arguments than the ones given here. We are not trying to prove too much here: simply that God (at least one) exists.

With these distinctions in mind, let us examine some proofs for God's existence. Saint Thomas Aquinas gave five distinct proofs for God's existence based upon common experience. For the sake of brevity, we will look only at the first, fourth, and fifth of the proofs he gave.

Proof 1: The First Unmoved Mover[44]

In this proof our nominal definition of God is "the first, unmoved mover." This may not at first sound like a good definition of God, but think about it: this would be the being which is the source of motion and action, which changes and acts upon other things, but is in no way changed or acted upon by anything else. If such a being can be shown to exist, it seems reasonable to call such a being God (or at least a god). Here's the proof:

---

[44] This proof corresponds to St. Thomas's first way.

1. Things in the world are in motion.

2. Everything in motion is moved by something else.

3. Therefore, there are things in the world moved by something else (i.e., there is a series of movers and moved things).

4. In every series of movers and moved things, either every mover is moved by another mover, or some first mover is not moved.

5. But not every mover is moved by another.

6. Therefore, there is a first, unmoved mover.

In the above argument, premises 2 and 5 still need to be proved. So here is the proof for them:

To prove premise 2, we need to recall the definition of motion: *the act of the potential insofar as it is potential.* From this it is clear that whatever is in motion begins in potency and ends in act. For example, whatever is heating up begins potentially hot and ends up actually hot. With this in mind, we can prove that everything in motion is moved by something else.

7. Either the things which begin in potency and end in act:

    a. give themselves act; or
    b. they are given act by something else.

But they cannot give themselves act (*a*) since:

8. Nothing gives more than it has, and

9. To have act is more than to have potency.

Therefore, nothing in potency gives itself act (not *a*).

Therefore, what begins in potency and ends in act is given act by something else (*b*). Therefore, everything which is in motion is moved by another thing.

The proof for premise (5) is:

If there are movers and things being moved by them in the world, then either:

a. everything which is a mover is itself moved; or
b. not every mover is moved by another thing.

If everything which is a mover is itself moved (*a*), then either:

c. there is an infinite series of moved movers; or
d. there is a circular series of moved movers.

But there cannot be an infinite series of moved movers (*c*), since, if there is no first mover, there won't be a middle or a last mover. For example, in a series of hangers, one must trace it back to something not hanging: an infinite number of hangers won't solve the problem. Or if light is reflected by many mirrors, there must be some first source of light that isn't reflected. An infinite number of mirrors won't solve the problem. Multiplying dependent movers does not make them less dependent, it only makes the problem worse!

Also, there cannot be a circular series of moved movers (*d*) (for example, A moves B which moves C which moves A), since this has the same problem. If hanger C is hanging from hanger B, and you explain the fact that hanger B doesn't fall because it is hanging from hanger A, and you explain that hanger A doesn't fall because it is hanging from hanger C, this is simply to avoid the problem: none of the hangers can stay up on their own. To say that the circular chain solves the problem is simply to assert that each of the hangers gives itself the power of not falling, but that is exactly what they don't have by definition. Something in motion does not have the power to move itself, to give itself something it doesn't have. Therefore, there cannot be a circular series of moved movers (*d*).

Consequently, not everything which is a mover is itself being moved (*a*). Therefore, not every mover is moved by another thing (*b*).

Our conclusion is that there must be a first, unmoved mover, and this is what we call God.

Proof 2: The First Cause of Goodness[45]

In this argument, our nominal definition of God is "the best thing which causes goodness in everything else." This is usually more readily admitted as a name for God than "the first unmoved mover." After all, if some best thing in the universe can be found which causes goodness in everything else, would it not deserve the name God? Here's the proof:

1. Things in the world are more or less good.
2. <u>But where things are more or less, there must be a most (at least one).</u>
3. Therefore, there must be something which is best (most good).
4. Those things that are less good are imperfectly good.
5. <u>What is imperfectly good must have a cause of its goodness.</u>

[45] This proof is similar to St. Thomas's fourth way.

6. Therefore, those things that are less good must have some cause of goodness.

7. Whatever has a cause of its goodness must get goodness from something better.

6. Those things that are less good have some cause of their goodness.
8. Therefore, those things that are less good get goodness from what is better.

Therefore, the best good (3) is also the cause of goodness in everything else (8). Hence, there exists a best thing which causes goodness in everything else.

However, premise 5 still needs to be proved.

If something has goodness, either:

a. it has goodness from itself; or

b. it has goodness from another.

If it has goodness from another (*b*), then it has goodness imperfectly, since it is better to have goodness on its own than to borrow it from another. On the other hand, if something has goodness from itself (*a*), then it must have goodness perfectly. For whatever has goodness from itself cannot cease to be good or even become less good, just as whatever has being from itself cannot cease to be. And this is to be good in the most perfect way.

Hence, whatever is imperfectly good must have some cause of its goodness, while whatever is perfectly good has no cause of its goodness (5). Our conclusion is that there exists a greatest good which causes goodness in all other things (i.e., God exists).

Proof 3: The Intelligence Which Governs Nature[46]

In this proof, our nominal definition of God is "the intelligent being which governs nature." Nearly all men accept this as the definition of God. Since we have already considered this argument in detail in chapters 8-10, we shall lay it out more succinctly here.

1. Whatever acts in an intelligent way always or for the most part either:
    a. has intelligence; or
    b. is governed by something having intelligence.
2. But all natural things act in an intelligent way always or for the most part and are not intelligent themselves.
3. Therefore, all natural things are governed by something having intelligence.

Therefore, there must be an intelligent being which governs nature, which is what we called God.

Someone might object to premise 2 by holding that natural things are not actually acting in an intelligent way, but only the appearance of intelligence is found in nature. We have already addressed this objection in chapters 8 through 10.

Someone might also object to premise 2 by denying that all natural things are not intelligent themselves, since obviously human beings are intelligent. But even human beings grow and develop in an intelligent way without being responsible for this. A human embryo develops eyes, ears, and a brain without being responsible for this by his own intelligence. So in fact all natural things are guided by some intelligence other than their own.

---

[46] This proof corresponds to St. Thomas's fifth way.

This concludes our course in natural philosophy. We have discovered that there is some kind of intelligence behind nature, an intelligence which is somehow akin to our own, but extending to the whole of nature. In the next book, we shall consider a very special kind of natural thing: living things, and in particular we shall consider the human soul, the principle of life in intelligent beings.

APPENDIX

Are Living Organisms Just Machines?[47]

It is commonplace to speak of living organisms as if they were complicated machines. This is quite understandable, since there are many significant similarities between most living organisms and machines. After all, if art imitates nature, one would expect that machines, the work of human art and ingenuity, would have correspondences to the structure of living organisms.

But are these likenesses such that whoever admits them would deserve to be called a "mechanist" (that is, someone who thinks that there are no significant differences between living organisms and machines)? Is it mechanistic to call the hip a ball-and-socket joint? Or is someone a mechanist if they assert that protein molecules are "built" within the cell, or that strands of DNA are "transcribed and copied"?

Let's begin by listing a number of clear likenesses between living organisms and machines:

[47] The author is indebted to Dr. Michael Augros for the content of this appendix.

1. Living organisms and machines are composed from many diverse parts.

2. The parts of a living organism, like those of a machine, are contained by a definite boundary to form a contiguous whole (e.g., by mutual contact or coherence).

3. The parts of a living organism, like those of a machine, work together in some order or arrangement by mutual interaction.

4. The parts of a living organism, like those of a machine, produce effects and properties which cannot be attributed to any one part, but only to many parts working in harmony (so-called "emergent properties"). For example, an airplane is flyable, even if each of its individual parts taken separately is not flyable.

None of these obvious likenesses require that a living organism is simply a kind of machine. Nor would any person who asserts these likenesses deserve to be called a mechanist. A mechanist is someone who asserts a further likeness:

5. The parts of a living thing, like those of a machine with moving parts, are distinct individual substances, and so the whole living thing is really a multitude of many interacting things, and not truly a single individual thing that is acting.

In other words, the mechanist asserts that a living organism, like a machine, is not really one substance, but many actual substances. This assertion is false (and even self-evidently false). Nevertheless, due to the intellectual customs of our age and the difficulties which arise concerning the status of the parts of a living organism, it is difficult for modern people to see that this assertion that living things are not one substance is false. I have dealt with many of these difficulties in chapter 6 above.

Here I simply call your attention to a simple fact of experience. The person who asserts that he knows that he is many substances finds himself in a quandary: who or what is the "he" that knows? The subject of any knowledge must be a single substance. Thus, the claim that each living thing is not one substance is self-defeating. So long as someone holds on to this basic fact of experience, that he is one substance acting in and through his many parts, the assertion that a living thing is merely a machine is untenable.